WILD
FLOWERS
of the
YUKON, ALASKA
& NORTHWESTERN
CANADA

WILD FLOWERS

of the
YUKON, ALASKA
& NORTHWESTERN
CANADA

John Trelawny

Harbour Publishing

Published by
Harbour Publishing Co. Ltd., P.O. Box 219, Madeira Park, BC V0N 2H0
www.harbourpublishing.com

Cover design Martin Nichols
Page design by Roger Handling
Front cover photo of fireweed (*Epilobium angustifolium*) and back cover photo of wild crocus (*Anemone patens* L.) by Wayne Towris
Page 2 photo of Arctic forget-me-not (*Eritrichium aretioides*) by R. Frisch
Illustrations by Paul Nystedt and Roger Handling
Map by John G. Callan and Roger Handling

Printed and bound in Canada

Harbour Publishing acknowledges the financial support from the Government of Canada through the Book Publishing Industry Development Program (BPIDP) and the Canada Council for the Arts, and the Province of British Columbia through the British Columbia Arts Council, for its publishing activities.

THE CANADA COUNCIL | LE CONSEIL DES ARTS
FOR THE ARTS | DU CANADA
SINCE 1957 | DEPUIS 1957

National Library of Canada Cataloguing in Publication Data

Trelawny, John G. S., 1919-
  Wild flowers of the Yukon, Alaska and northwestern Canada

  Previously published under title: Wildflowers of the Yukon, Alaska and northwestern Canada.
  Includes index.
  ISBN 1-55017-257-3

  1. Wild flowers—Yukon Territory—Identification. 2. Wild flowers—Northwest Territories—Mackenzie—Identification. 3. Wild flowers—British Columbia, Northern—Identification. 4. Wild flowers—Alaska—Identification. I. Title. II. Title: Trelawny, John G. S., 1919- Wildflowers of the Yukon, Alaska and northwestern Canada.
QK203.Y8T74 2003   582.13'09719'1   C2001-911665-9
QK203.Y8T74 2003   582.13'09719'1   C2001-911665-9

The work of putting together this field guide was to a large extent a team effort due to the boundless generosity of many friends. Foremost amongst these is Robert Frisch, for, besides making available his magnificent collection of coloured photographs, he imparted freely his vast knowledge of the flora of the Yukon, the result of many years of study in the area. I also extend my deepest gratitude to Norman Barichello, who so generously put his valuable photographic collection—compiled during his years of biological study in the north—at my disposal, and I am no less grateful to the memory of Mr. and Mrs. W. Ken Dobson who donated so much of their time, energy and photographic skill in helping to record the wild flowers of the Yukon and northern BC. I would also like to mention the late Mr. and Mrs. T. Armstrong and Mrs. J.M. Woollett, who so generously made their collections of photographs available to me. I am, as well, most grateful to the many others who so kindly contributed such excellent coloured photographs from their collections, duly mentioned on the page of credits.

I am deeply indebted to Dr. J.E. McInerney, former Chairman of the Department of Biology, University of Victoria, whose confidence in the outcome of this project, demonstrated by his encouragement and material support, played a large part in making it a viable undertaking. Amongst others who were helpful I would especially like to thank Dr. Geraldine Allen for donating so much of her time and showing such a deep interest, giving most valuable advice on many matters concerning the text and the illustrations. I am most grateful to Dr. Adolf Ceska for reading through and advising on the text, and to Dr. Nancy J. Turner as well as the late Dr. E.H. Lohbrunner for their interest and encouragement.

Thanks go also to Dr. Bruce Bennett of the Yukon Fish and Wildlife Branch for the input of his expertise on northern flora, and also to David Murray for his advice in this area.

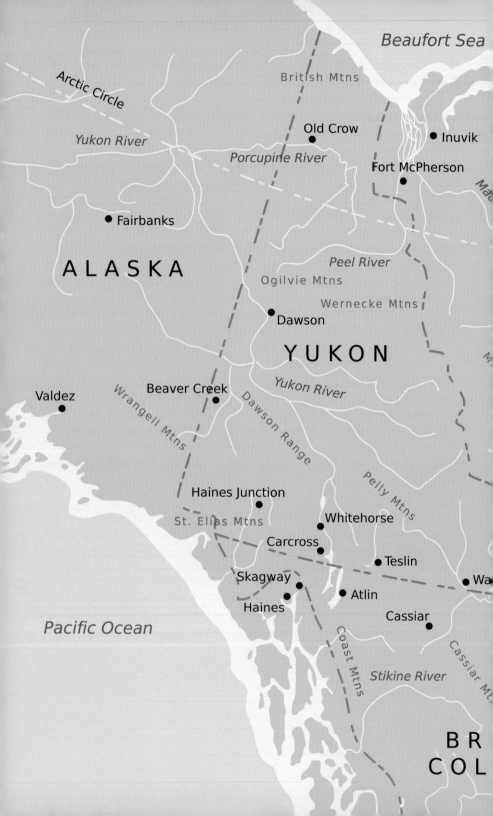

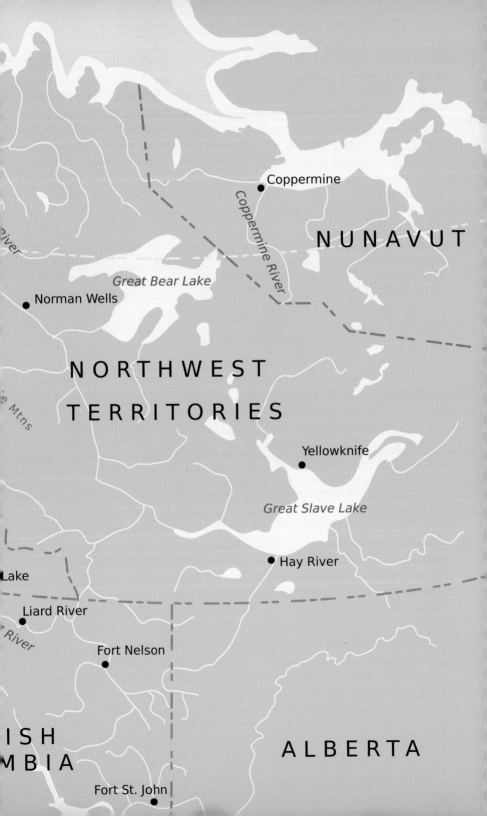

The aim of this book is to fulfil the need for a popular guide to the flowering plants of the Yukon and its adjacent areas. No attempt has been made to produce a complete catalogue of all the plant species that have been found there. Instead, representatives of nearly all the families of flowering plants that are likely to be encountered in northwest Canada and neighbouring Alaska have been illustrated and described. The purpose has been to make the book comprehensive enough to suit a wide range of users without it becoming too cumbersome. May it be an enjoyable possession of many households and stimulate an interest in wild flowers generally, and a concern for the preservation of the environment.

Plant species have been included in their recognized families, and they are arranged according to the Englerian sequence of plant families, a convention that is commonly used by many botanists. Thus, the locating of plant species in the book should be quite straightforward for the experienced plant hunter. However, for the less experienced, a simple key involving flower colour and shape is included. Within this key, the plants are listed in the order in which they occur in the book, so the search is quickly narrowed down in most cases to the perusal of a few coloured pictures to determine the exact species.

It is often difficult to select English names for plant species without ambiguity or duplication. The problem is especially evident in a book such as this one that covers a vast area, and includes many plants that are circumboreal in range. The use of Latin names precludes such confusion. However, since the English names are important to many interested plant hunters, the binomial Latin name of the genus and species *and* the English or colloquial names have been included in every case.

The description that accompanies the illustration of each species is in most cases limited to structures that are easily observable without a magnifying glass and in these descriptions the use of technical botanical terms has been kept to a minimum. However, in some cases, laborious wordy explanations have been eliminated by the use of conventional botanical terms, and an illustrated glossary has been added to explain these. This glossary is also intended to assist the less experienced in understanding flower and leaf structure and shape.

Since flowering times vary so much according to altitude, latitude or other ecological conditions, and since the growing season is so short in the north, no attempt has been made to add this information for all species.

Accompanying each illustration is a description of the range of that species: its distribution within the area covered by this book, including the Yukon, the District of Mackenzie, northern British Columbia as far south as 55° North Latitude, and eastern Alaska. This region is shown on the map and is referred to frequently in the text as "our area."

This book is dedicated to the memory of Robert Frisch, who contributed so much and who passed away in the Yukon in June 1985.

John Trelawny, Victoria, BC

SCHEUCHZERIACEAE
Arrow-grass Family

SEASIDE ARROW-GRASS

Triglochin maritima L.

An obliquely ascending rootstock, covered with whitish leaf bases and several linear, fleshy leaves, gives rise to smooth flower stems that may be up to 1 m (3 ft.) tall, though they are usually much shorter. The flowers are small, with greenish sepals and petals. It may be found in meadows and saline marshes inland as well as on the coast. Circumpolar in range, it extends through scattered areas of Alas., s. Yukon and n. BC, and most of the Dist. of Mackenzie.

CYPERACEAE Sedge Family

WHITE COTTON GRASS

Eriophorum scheuchzeri Hoppe

This often forms pure stands of solitary stems up to 30 cm (12 in.) high, with one or two clasping leaves near the base, that rise from a thin, creeping rootstock. The cotton grasses, consisting of some six or seven species in our area, are conspicuous and well known by their white perianth bristles, which form a white woolly tuft at the top of the stem. Sometimes acres of these woolly heads may be seen covering marshy, peaty places, often in shallow water around the edges of ponds, during the summer months. This species is circumpolar and is not uncommon throughout our area n. of 60° N.L.

POACEAE Grass Family

FOX-TAIL BARLEY
Hordeum jubatum L.

The erect stems, 30–40 cm (12–16 in.) tall, with two or three long thin leaves 3–5 mm (1/8–3/16 in.) wide, each bear a nodding, pale green to purple spike that may be up to 10 cm (4 in.) long. Grasses have two unique bracts surrounding each flower called "glumes"; inside these are structures called the "lemma" and the "palea." In barley the glume is long and slender, and the lemma is tipped with a slender bristle up to 8 cm (3 in.) in length that is called an "awn." Barley is easily recognized by these long awns, which give a silky, almost fluid, appearance to the heads of fox-tail barley as they wave in unison in the breeze. This close relative of our cultivated barley (*H. vulgare* L.) is an attractive sight on sandy soil, on river banks, in disturbed areas and on roadsides. Common in the Yukon River drainage system throughout c. Alas. and in s.w. Yukon, it also abounds in disturbed regions in the Mackenzie River valley, extending n. to the delta and e. around Great Slave Lake.

LILIACEAE Lily Family

WILD CHIVES
Allium schoenoprasum L.

The ovoid bulbs occur in clusters and are covered with a white, papery membrane. Long, thin, tapering leaves, shorter than the flower stalk, are half-round in cross-section and hollow near the base. The numerous flowers are compacted into a dense, nearly spherical umbel and have pink or rose-violet perianth segments with darker veins. This attractive ancestor of the cultivated chive is found around the world in northern regions of the northern hemisphere in damp grassy meadows, generally flowering

in late June or early July according to the elevation. Both leaves and bulbs are edible and make a very acceptable substitute for the garden variety.

INDIAN RICE, CHOCOLATE LILY, KAMCHATKA FRITILLARY, SARANA, NORTHERN RICE-ROOT

Fritillaria camschatcensis (L.) Ker-Gawl. This is the only fritillary found in our area. The sturdy, branchless stems grow up to 42 cm (17 in.) tall with the lower leaves borne in two or three whorls. Flowers, a brownish purple, are pendant and bell-like with slightly flared petals and sepals. The name "rice-root" or "Indian rice" refers to the bulbs that are found 3–5 cm (1 1/4–2 in.) underground. Covered with fleshy scales that have the appearance of clusters of cooked rice grains, they are nutritious, and have been used as a source of winter food by many Native peoples. Indian rice is a plant mainly of the coastal mountains of BC and Alas., and it may be found in the Haines and White Pass regions.

ALPINE LILY

Lloydia serotina (L.) Rchb.
The pale cream corolla is delicately pink-flushed below and purple-veined above, the mid-vein prominent. About 12 mm (1/2 in.) wide, it is usually carried singly at the top of a slender stalk that may be up to 20 cm (8 in.) tall. A few of the long, narrow, fleshy leaves occur along the stem, though most are basal, arising from a thick, creeping rootstock. The Alp lily is a feature of high rocky slopes, dry grassy meadows, heathlands and arctic tundra throughout Alas., n. BC and the Yukon, extending e. to the Richardson and Mackenzie Mtns.

CLASPING TWISTED STALK

Streptopus amplexifolius (L.) DC.

"Amplexifolius" means "clasping leaf." The ovate leaves clasp the 30–120 cm (1–4 ft.) branched stem. Small, pale, greenish-yellow flowers have strongly reflexed petals and sepals. Each one hangs from a curiously kinked, slender stalk, providing a very distinctive recognition feature. The numerous attractive berries are bright red and are edible. Young shoots can also be eaten raw, but great care should be taken not to confuse these with the shoots of very poisonous *Veratrum eschscholtzii* (which see). It is found in moist woodlands in scattered locations over s. Yukon, the upper Liard valley and other areas in n. BC up to moderate altitudes.

STAR-FLOWERED SOLOMON'S SEAL
Maianthemum stellatum (L.) Link

The unbranched stems, up to 60 cm (24 in.) high, bear 7–13 strongly veined, alternately arranged, lanceolate leaves that may be up to 18 cm (7 in.) long and finely hairy underneath; above these about 10 small, white, starlike flowers are rather widely spaced from the tip. They appear in midsummer and are followed by greenish berries that turn red in the fall. The stems arise from far-ranging rootstocks, forming rather dense colonies in open damp meadows. It ranges through s.w. Yukon, n. BC, and the upper Mackenzie drainage system; it is also reported from a few locations in south-central Alas. Another species, THREE-LEAVED SOLOMON'S SEAL, *M. trifolium* (L.) Sloboda, occurs in s.e. Yukon and n.e. BC. This is a less robust plant. In spite of its name, it may bear two, three or four leaves, though usually three—elliptical in shape and smooth on the underside. The small white flowers are borne well above the leaves. It is found in more acid conditions in bogs and peaty soil in s.e. Yukon, and the upper Mackenzie drainage system.

NORTHERN FALSE ASPHODEL
Tofieldia coccinea Richards.

This is a small, inconspicuous plant, rarely more than 15 cm (6 in.) tall. One, occasionally two, clasping leaves on the stem distinguish this from *T. pusilla* (which see). The numerous basal leaves usually form a dense clump. Flowers are white or cream to dark red, pink in bud and in fruit. They are arranged in a compact raceme, which elongates in fruit. In tundra and rather dry, rocky, alpine situations, this little plant may be found through n. and s.w. Yukon, extreme n.w. BC, the Mackenzie River valley and in most of Alas.

WESTERN FALSE ASPHODEL

Triantha glutinosa (Michx.) Baker
This is a plant of marshes and
swamps. It has a stout, glandular
(sticky) stem, 12–35 cm (4 3/4–14
in.) tall, and broadly linear leaves
more than half this length. The
sepals and petals are creamy white;
these are followed by erect, plump,
reddish-purple capsules that are
about 6 mm (1/4 in.) long. This
species extends from s. coastal Alas.
e. It occurs in n.w. and n.e. BC, in c.
and s.e. Yukon and throughout the
Mackenzie River drainage system s.
of the delta.

SCOTCH ASPHODEL,
FALSE ASPHODEL

Tofieldia pusilla (Michx.) Pers.
Green stems up to 25 cm (10 in.) tall are leafless (or have one small, poorly
developed leaf near the base). The basal leaves, numerous and densely tufted,
are not more than 10 cm (4 in.) long. Terminal clusters of white to greenish
flowers are followed by green fruit 1.5–3 mm (1/8 in.) long. This is a plant
of wetter sites than *T. coccinea* (which see), and it may be found in moist,
calcareous, turfy places up to 1,500 m (5,000 ft.) throughout our area.

FALSE HELLEBORE
Veratrum eschscholtzii Gray

Considered a subspecies of *V. viride* Ait. by some authors, this conspicuously tall perennial (up to 2.5 m /7 1/2 ft. high) is found in wet meadows in montane and occasionally lowland regions. Large, coarse, clasping leaves are heavily ribbed and the insignificant flowers on drooping branches are greenish-yellow. They open June–September, according to altitude. These plants provide a striking accent in subalpine regions in s. Yukon, the Mackenzie Mtns. and throughout n. BC. They contain a poisonous alkaloid that may prove fatal if eaten.

ELEGANT POISON CAMAS, MOUNTAIN DEATH CAMAS, WHITE CAMAS
Zigadenus elegans Pursh

Bulbs give rise to a cluster of grassy leaves, both basal and on the 15–40 cm (6–16 in.) flower stems. Open, symmetrical racemes bear creamy-white flowers. Each of the six petals has a greenish-yellow honey gland at its base. The name is apt as this plant contains the poisonous alkaloid zygadine which, if eaten, causes vomiting, lowered body temperature, difficult breathing and, finally, coma. This species of death camas is widely distributed in poplar forests and open, grassy meadows

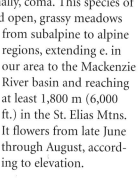

from subalpine to alpine regions, extending e. in our area to the Mackenzie River basin and reaching at least 1,800 m (6,000 ft.) in the St. Elias Mtns. It flowers from late June through August, according to elevation.

IRIDACEAE Iris Family

BLUE-EYED GRASS

Sisyrinchium montanum Greene

This is a tufted, grass-like herb growing from a short rootstock. The stem, 20–30 cm (8–12 in.) tall, is flattened and wing-margined. Leaves, which are few and basal, are about half as long as the stem. Flowers are borne in a few-flowered inflorescence (the picture taken near Haines Junction shows a single flower) and they are 1.5–2 cm (5/8–3/4 in.) wide. This species is found in open, dry, sometimes alkaline, meadows.

ORCHIDACEAE Orchid Family

ONE-LEAF ORCHID, ROUND-LEAF ORCHID, FLY-SPECKLED ORCHID

Amerorchis rotundifolia (Banks) Hult.

Syn. *Orchis rotundifolia* Banks

"Rotundifolia" (round-leaved) refers to the single leaf, which is in fact slightly egg-shaped and sometimes as much as 8 cm (3 in.) long. A slender, 20–30 cm (8–12 in.) stem bears two to eight white or pale rose-coloured flowers in a spaced flower spike. Each has a very prominent lip, which is three-lobed; the long terminal lobe expanded and two-cleft, with conspicuous rose-purple spots. The delicate blooms appear in late June and in July in damp forests and on stream banks. It ranges throughout the Yukon—except the extreme north—n. BC and the upper Mackenzie River drainage area and extends s.e. into c. BC.

CALYPSO, FAIRY SLIPPER, LADY'S SLIPPER, FALSE LADY'S SLIPPER

Calypso bulbosa (L.) Oakes

"Calypso" (the sea-nymph daughter of Atlas) means "concealment," referring to the habit of this attractive flower of hiding amongst mosses in the deep shade of dense forests. The single leaf is firm, oval and corrugated; it appears in late summer, overwintering and persisting until after the flower bud is pushed up by the 5–20 cm (2–8 in.) flower stalk in May or June, when the leaf slowly withers. The blossom has three sepals and two petals, all delicate mauve, above the jewel-like lip or "slipper," and its fragrance is quite distinctive. It is found in the Yukon and in n. BC from the Coast Mtns. to the upper Mackenzie River drainage system and around Great Bear and Great Slave lakes in the NWT.

NORTHERN CORAL-ROOT

Corallorhiza trifida Chat.

This plant lacks green leaves; instead, the yellowish-green 10–30 cm (4–12 in.)-tall stem usually has two long brown sheaths for half its length. The rather open raceme bears a few tiny flowers, having yellowish-green petals and sepals. The lip is whitish, often spotted with magenta. The species name, *trifida*, refers to the three lobes of the lip. The coral-like rhizome is brittle, lacking roots. A circumpolar plant, it can be found all through our area at various locations in forests, and in the open tundra n. of the treeline.

YELLOW LADY'S SLIPPER, YELLOW MOCCASIN FLOWER

Cypripedium parviflorum Salisb.
Syn. *C. calceolus* L.

This showy orchid bears its single (rarely two to three) elegant and perfumed blossoms on a 15–20 cm (6–8 in.) stalk above broad and conspicuously veined leaves. The upper sepal and two linear, lateral petals are greenish-yellow to purplish-brown, and the latter, up to 4 cm (1 1/2 in.) long, are spirally twisted. The showy, inflated "pouch" is golden yellow. It often grows in clumps in moist, open woodland, mossy swamps or mountain slopes, flowering May–August according to location. The species is found in the Liard and upper Mackenzie River drainage systems in n.e. BC, the Dist. of Mackenzie, in extreme n.w. BC, and in a few scattered localities in c. and n. Yukon.

PINK LADY'S SLIPPER
Cypripedium guttatum Sw.
This attractive orchid has a conspicuous 2 cm (3/4 in.) "pouch" that, with the two ovate lateral petals, is highly variable in colour, but generally is pink or white with purple and greenish-purple blotches. The 10–30 cm (4–12 in.) stem, with two ovate leaves at about the middle, rises from a slender rootstock and bears a single flower subtended by a leafy bract. Truly a northern species, it is rare and localized in open mossy woods and meadows along the Yukon River, the Alaska–Yukon border n. of Beaver Creek, and in the Peel and Mackenzie River basins.

SPARROW'S EGG LADY'S SLIPPER, NORTHERN LADY'S SLIPPER
Cypripedium passerinum Richards.
The solitary flowers with short, greenish sepals and whitish petals rounded at the ends have an egg-shaped "pouch" about 2 cm (3/4 in.) long. It is white or pale magenta with bright purple spots on the interior wall; these sometimes show

faintly on the outside. The large clasping leaves and the stem, up to 35 cm (14 in.) high, are densely hairy. This plant is found through most of c. Alas., throughout n. BC, and the Yukon to treeline, and the Yukon and upper Mackenzie River drainage systems, usually blooming in late June or early July in sphagnum bogs, gravel outwashes and wet talus. Another white-flowered *Cypripedium*, MOUNTAIN LADY'S SLIPPER, *C. montanum* Dougl., has been located in extreme n.w. BC. Its flowers are sweet-scented, and it has thin, pointed petals that are spirally twisted.

NORTHERN RATTLESNAKE PLANTAIN
Goodyera repens (L.) R.Br.

A creeping, branching rootstock gives rise to basal rosettes of leaves that are petiolate and ovate-lanceolate in shape, about 2–3 cm (3/4–1 3/16 in.) long. One variety has leaves in which the veins are bordered with pale tissue lacking chlorophyll so that, contrasting with the green tissue of the leaf, they form a conspicuous network. These and another variety, with leaves that are green throughout, may sometimes be found growing side by side. The tiny, greenish-white flowers are borne in a one-sided raceme 15–25 cm (6–10 in.) tall. This is a plant of damp, mossy woodlands. It extends from c. Alas. e. through most of our area s. of the Arctic Circle and s.e. in the Rockies.

NORTHERN TWAYBLADE
Listera borealis Morong

The smooth stem is slightly four-sided, rarely as much as 20–25 cm (8–10 in.) high. Just above the middle of the stem is an opposite pair of rather large, thin, oval to elliptical leaves. The tiny flowers usually number less than 12, spaced in an open raceme. They are pale yellowish-green, with petals showing a darker mid-vein. The lip is disproportionately long, wider at the tip (which is shallowly notched) with a distinctive pair of minute, ear-like structures at its narrow base. It is found in cool, moist woods throughout our area, s. in the Rockies.

HEART-LEAF TWAYBLADE
Listera cordata (L.) R.Br.
This 10–30 cm (4–12 in.) slender plant holds its twin leaves above the moss in bogs and coniferous forests from Alas. to Ore. It is circumboreal, but in our area it is confined to s. Yukon and n. BC. Some species have greenish flowers; in others they may be dark purple to blackish. They are easily identified by the uniquely forked lip.

TALL WHITE BOG ORCHID
Platanthera dilatata (Pursh) Lindley
Syn. *Habenaria dilatata* (Pursh) Hook.
This has an impressive single stem up to 1 m (3 ft.) tall, the top quarter of which is covered with gleaming white flowers. As many as 20 of these irregular blooms may be open on a stem at one time. Each one is almost 2.5 cm (1 in.) wide, and has a spur-like projection from behind the distinctive "lip" (lower petal). The smooth stem is clasped by rather succulent leaves that are spearhead-shaped below but become smaller and more slender upward. This species exudes a most striking fragrance. It can be seen in bogs, and on stream banks and lake shores along the s. Alas. coast, through s. Yukon, the Mackenzie Mtns. and n. BC.

GREEN-FLOWERED BOG ORCHID, NORTHERN GREEN ORCHID

Platanthera aquilonis Sheviak
Syn. *P. hyperborea auct. non* (L.) Lindl.
Syn. *Habenaria hyperborea* (L.) R.Br.
This plant is usually less than 50 cm (20 in.) tall with yellowish-green flowers, each having a distinctive curved spur and tapering pointed lip, crowded in a 7–10 cm (3–4 in.) raceme. They are smaller than those of *P. dilatata* (which see). The lanceolate, clasping leaves become progressively smaller up the stem. Blooming in June or July, this bog orchid ranges from Alas. to Greenland. It is quite common in bogs, marshes and lake shores in n. BC, s.w. Yukon and in the Yukon and Mackenzie River drainage systems.

ONE-LEAVED REIN ORCHID, SMALL NORTHERN BOG ORCHID

Platanthera obtusata (Pursh) Lindley
Syn. *Habenaria obtusata* (Pursh) Richards.
The single 8–13 cm (3–5 in.) blunt-tipped leaf is often partly hidden in the moss of forests, bogs, swamps, or even grassy slopes; nor is the 15–25 cm (6–10 in.) flower stem, with its greenish-yellow flowers, easily seen. The flower spur is slightly curved and tapered. The leaf is usually more than twice as long as it is wide. This is quite a common species throughout most of our area up to at least 900 m (3,000 ft.), blooming from about mid-June through early July.

HOODED LADIES' TRESSES
Spiranthes romanzoffiana Cham.
The small, greenish-white, faintly perfumed flowers are closely packed in three spiral ranks, like neatly braided hair. The parallel-veined leaves are chiefly basal, though a few small ones appear on the 10–40 cm (4–16 in.) unbranched stem. Its range is extensive, in moist places in fields and swamps, up to 900 m (3,000 ft.) in our area.

SALICACEAE Willow Family

ARCTIC WILLOW
Salix arctica Pall.
Some 50 species of willows, many of them dwarf in habit, may be found in our area. Identification of many of these is often difficult even for the expert. Representing the group is a commonly seen species that is a prostrate, mat-forming plant, usually 5–10 cm (2–4 in.) high, although it may reach 1 m (3 ft.) in the Aleutians. The leaves, elliptic to obovate, are 2.5–7 cm (1–2 3/4 in.) long and 1.5–2.5 cm (5/8–1 in.) wide, with entire margins. They are dull green, smooth on the upper surface and slightly pubescent below when young. Male catkins are easily recognized by their bright red anthers. The pistillate (female) catkins, 3–6 cm (1 3/16–2 1/4 in.) long, have dark brown or blackish-tipped scales that enclose the flowers with long hairs. This species is circumpolar and occurs on arctic and alpine tundra throughout our area.

MYRICACEAE
Wax Myrtle Family

SWEET GALE
Myrica gale L.

This is a medium-sized, deciduous shrub, seldom more than 1 m (3 ft.) tall. The 3–5 cm (1–2 in.)-long, oblanceolate, greyish leaves are sparsely toothed toward the tip. They give off a strong aroma from many bright yellow wax glands. Inconspicuous flowers are borne in catkins; the male catkins—about 2 cm (3/4 in.) long—are about twice the length of the female ones, and they are on separate shrubs. Sweet gale appears on wet lake shores and in muskeg and black spruce bogs in central Yukon, along the e. side of the Mackenzie River valley and around Great Bear and Great Slave lakes.

BETULACEAE Birch Family

MOUNTAIN ALDER
Alnus crispa (Ait.) Pursh

A bushy shrub up to 3 m (9 ft.) high, often forming dense thickets. The leaves are ovate to elliptic, smooth on top and hairy on the veins beneath. Leaf margins are irregularly serrulate with sharp teeth. Flowers develop with the leaves on the new growth each spring, male flowers borne in pendant catkins. The female catkins are shorter and wider, giving rise to ovoid, woody, cone-like structures.

Mountain alder is common throughout our area in tundra and open woodland, and on mountain slopes and stream banks. Another species, GREY ALDER, *A. incana* (L.) Moench, is often taller and more tree-like, sometimes reaching heights of 5 m (15 ft.) or more. It has serrate leaf-margins that are sometimes shallowly lobed. The flowers develop before the leaves in spring. It may be found along stream banks in the Yukon and Mackenzie River valleys.

SANTALACEAE
Sandalwood Family

RED-FRUITED BASTARD TOAD-FLAX, NORTHERN COMANDRA

Geocaulon lividum (Richards.) Fern.
Syn. *Comandra livida* Richards.
This low, 10–25 cm (4–10 in.) shrub growing from spreading rhizomes is found throughout our area and across boreal America in mossy open woods. It bears single or a few inconspicuous, purplish-green, five-sepalled flowers in the axils of elliptical leaves. Small, 5 mm (3/16 in.) or less, they lack petals, and yield a bright orange-red fruit that is edible, but not palatable. A species of the closely related genus, BASTARD TOAD-FLAX, *Comandra pallida* A. DC., from rather drier sites, has been located in c. Yukon and n.e. BC. It is taller, with clusters of pale yellow flowers, and the fruit is blue to purplish when ripe.

POLYGONACEAE Buckwheat Family

MOUNTAIN SORREL

Oxyria digyna (L.) Hill
Smooth, slightly fleshy leaves with long petioles are distinctive, being kidney-shaped to heart-shaped, often reddish (especially below). From the basal tuft of leaves several stems, 10–30 cm (4–12 in.) tall, carry crowded panicles of minute greenish flowers. These are soon succeeded by a cluster of conspicuous, reddish, broadly winged, oval fruit, each about 1 cm (3/8 in.) long. The sharply sour leaves are edible, but the root is not.
Mountain sorrel may be found up to 3,700 m (12,000 ft.) in the mountains from Alas. e. to the Richardson and Mackenzie Mtns., and throughout the Arctic.

WILD RHUBARB
Polygonum alaskanum (Small) Wight

A shrubby plant with hollow branching stems up to 2 m (6 ft.) tall rises from a woody rhizome. Leaves, more or less sessile, or on short petioles, are up to 20 cm (8 in.) long, lanceolate to ovate and tapering to a fine point. The widely branching inflorescence is a mass of tiny yellowish-white flowers. It usually grows in large showy clumps, often on roadsides and newly exposed clay banks, throughout most of Alas., except the n. and s. coastal regions, and through c. and n. Yukon e. to the Mackenzie Mtns. and the Mackenzie River delta. The succulent young stems and leaves are edible.

WATER SMARTWEED
Polygonum amphibium L.

Leaves up to 15 cm (6 in.) long are oblong-lanceolate and arranged alternately up the smooth stem. Thin wisps of roots commonly grow from the leaf axils. The stem ends in a spike-like, tight panicle of dozens of small pinkish-red flowers. Water smartweed occurs in ponds and wet places at low elevations throughout the Yukon and Mackenzie River systems.

BISTORT
Polygonum bistorta L.

A sturdy spike, up to 50 cm (20 in.) tall, bears a showy cluster of small, bright pink flowers. Basal leaves are elongated with a rather wedge-shaped base and winged petioles. Found in moist meadows and tundra, it ranges from w. and n. Yukon and the Mackenzie delta w. through Alas. The sturdy rhizome and leaves are edible.

ALPINE BISTORT
Polygonum viviparum L.
Syn. *Bistorta vivipara* (L.) S.F. Gray

A perennial plant with a solitary, 10–30 cm (4–12 in.) stem, it bears one or two narrow, sessile leaves. The stem terminates in a spike (up to 10 cm/4 in. long) of white (or pinkish) flowers, the lower ones replaced by bulblets that sometimes grow into small plants before they fall. The stem rises from a cluster of long-petioled, linear to lanceolate, shiny, dark green leaves on a short, twisted rootstock. It was eaten by the Inuit and is said to taste like almonds. Circumpolar, alpine bistort is common throughout our area in moist or sometimes dry meadows and open places up to 2,000 m (6,600 ft.).

ARCTIC DOCK

Rumex arcticus Trautv.

Stems, sometimes bright red, grow to a height of 100 cm (40 in.) or more, and terminate in a panicle of small reddish flowers. Leaves, mostly basal, are lanceolate to oblong-ovate, rounded at the tip and up to 30 cm (12 in.) long. They are dark green and slightly fleshy, and have been extensively collected, boiled and preserved for winter use by Native people. It is locally common in damp, open places over most of the Yukon, the Mackenzie delta and n.e. BC; it also grows throughout Alas.

CHENOPODIACEAE Goosefoot Family

STRAWBERRY BLITE
Chenopodium capitatum (L.) Asch.
Bright crimson, rounded clusters of fruit in the axils of the leaves make this species easily recognizable from June onwards. It is a well-branched plant, rarely more than 70 cm (28 in.) tall in the north. The leaves, more or less triangular and up to 10 cm (4 in.) long, may be eaten boiled when young. It is common on gravel bars and in disturbed regions over most of our area except in the far north.

PORTULACACEAE Purslane Family

TUBEROUS SPRING-BEAUTY
Claytonia tuberosa Pall.
Slender brittle stems, 10–15 cm (4–6 in.) high, rise from a more or less spherical, edible corm up to 1.5 cm (5/8 in.) in diameter, often deeply underground. A pair of opposite, sessile, lanceolate leaves is borne on the stem, and there may be a few, long-petioled basal leaves. Three to five white or (rarely) pink flowers, the petals having a yellowish base, are borne in a loose corymb at the top of the stem. The seeds are black and shiny. Found in moist places in tundra or rocky mountain slopes in c. Yukon and the c. Yukon River valley of e. Alas., it also occurs in the mountains of s.e. and s.w. Yukon, extreme n.w. BC, disjunctly in the Mackenzie and Richardson Mtns. and in extreme n.e. Alas.

CARYOPHYLLACEAE
Pink Family

MOUSE-EAR CHICKWEED
Cerastium arvense L.

Leaves and stems are usually covered with white hairs, though less so in montane situations. The flowers may be nearly 2 cm (3/4 in.) wide. Petals are cleft about one-third of their length, and marked with greenish lines that serve as honey guides. The five hairy sepals, about half the length of the petals, are lanceolate-pointed. There are 10 stamens. This far-ranging and variable species is common throughout temperate N. Amer. It ranges into s.e. Alas. and is found in s. Yukon, n. along the c. Yukon River and in the Mackenzie River valley and foothills to the delta. It may be found on river bars and in dry to moist meadows up to subalpine levels.

GREATER CHICKWEED

Cerastium maximum L.

Solitary stems, or a few in clumps, up to 70 cm (28 in.) tall, have several pairs of opposite leaves that are ovate-lanceolate. The terminal inflorescence bears usually three to nine showy white flowers. Petals, 2 cm (3/4 in.) long, are cleft for about a quarter of their length. This is the most attractive and distinctive species of *Cerastium* in our area and it may be found in thickets, open woods, gravel bars or meadows in n. and central-western Yukon and adjacent Alas.

SEABEACH SANDWORT

Honckenya peploides (L.) Ehrh.
This is a plant of sandy sea shores.
The smooth, branching and freely
rooting stems are often partially
buried in sand, with upright
shoots that can be up to 25 cm (10
in.) tall. Many yellow-green, ovate
to lanceolate, fleshy leaves are
arranged in opposite pairs along
the stem, becoming more crowded
towards the tip. The flowers, borne
in the upper leaf axils, have four or
five sepals and an equal number of

petals, both about the same length. The flowers are often dioecious, having only
male or female parts fully developed. Found quite commonly along the Pacific
coast from the Bering Strait s., it is circumpolar and ranges all along the Arctic
coast of our area. This plant is named for the 18th-century botanist Gerhard
Honckeny.

ARCTIC CATCHFLY

Silene involucrata (Cham. &
Schlect.) Bocquet
Syn. *Melandrium affine* J. Vahl
Syn. *Lychnis furcata* Fern.
From a basal rosette of
oblanceolate leaves erect stems
rise 5–30 cm (2–12 in.) high.
These have one or two pairs of
opposite lanceolate leaves, and
two or three erect flowers. Five
milk-white cleft petals extend
for one-third to one-half of
their length beyond the
striped calyx. This is a plant of
sandy, gravelly places. It is circumpolar in range; in our area
it is quite common in Arctic
alpine regions, with isolated
occurrences in the Mackenzie
Mtns.

BLADDER CAMPION, APETALOUS CAMPION

Silene uralensis (Rupr.) Bocquet
Syn. *Melandrium apetalum* (L.) Fenzl.
Syn. *Lychnis apetala* L.
Linear leaves, about 4 cm (1 1/2 in.) long, crowd the base of the unbranched flower stems that are up to 20 cm (8 in.) tall, and have one or two pairs of sessile leaves. The solitary nodding flower has an inflated, bladder-like calyx, which is purple-striped, giving it the appearance of a miniature Japanese lantern. In spite of the name "apetalous" (without petals), these can be seen, lilac-coloured, protruding slightly beyond the calyx. After flowering, the seed capsule is erect. Found on moist grassy slopes or in mossy places, it is circumpolar and fairly common throughout our area at moderately high elevations.

LONG-PODDED SANDWORT

Minuartia macrocarpa (Pursh) Ostenf.
This is a loosely tufted plant with trailing branches that are covered with soft, flat, usually linear leaves. The leaf-margins are lined with small hairs. Single flowers have white petals that are about twice as long as the green, softly pubescent sepals. The distinctive oblong seed capsule is 15–18 mm (5/8 in.) long when mature. It is found on rocky slopes and well-drained alpine tundra, ranging e. through the mountains of Alas. and the Yukon to the Mackenzie Mtns.

LARCH-LEAVED SANDWORT
Minuartia yukonensis Hult.
A loose tuft, up to 40 cm (16 in.) broad, arises from a taproot and a much-branched caudex. These short branches are covered in small, needle-like leaves. Flowering stems, up to 17 cm (6 3/4 in.) tall, bear one or two flowers with white, 1 cm (3/8 in.)-long petals about 1 1/2 times longer than the sepals. This sandwort has been found in scattered locations in Alas. and the Yukon, and is known in the area around Dawson, where it is locally quite common in disturbed, dry gravelly places, especially on Midnight Dome, at Dawson City.

MOSS CAMPION
Silene acaulis (L.) Jacq.

Incredibly tight cushions, like patches of moss, up to 30 cm (12 in.) wide, can be found pressed flat over the rock, their long woody taproots deeply anchored in crevices. Tiny leaves on much-branched stems are tough, leathery and linear. These bright green mats become spangled with tight-pressed, bright rose-coloured flowers throughout the summer. This is an extremely variable circumpolar species. It is found throughout our area quite commonly in the Arctic regions, up to 2,000 m (6,600 ft.) in well-drained gravelly or rocky places.

PINK CAMPION
Silene repens Patrin

An often solitary, pubescent stem, up to 50 cm (20 in.) tall, bears five or more opposite pairs of sessile leaves up to 6 cm (2 3/8 in.) long. This is topped by a branched inflorescence, sometimes rather congested. The tubular calyx is purplish and finely pubescent, and the white petals (sometimes pink), about twice as long as the calyx, are deeply cleft. Pink campion is locally abundant in sandy or gravelly open places, in open willow thickets, or on rocky slopes and subalpine forests in the n., c. and w. regions of the Yukon and adjacent Alas., and the n.w. Dist. of Mackenzie.

LONG-STALKED STARWORT, CHICKWEED
Stellaria longipes Goldie

Some 10 species of chickweed range through our area; many are circumboreal and widespread. They are found in moist places, on stony slopes in the mountains and on tundra. They are generally quite similar and often variable; however, long-stalked starwort is illustrated as being fairly typical of the genus. Generally, the starworts (or chickweeds) are perennial herbs, with either prostrate or upright stems that bear small, sessile and opposite leaves. Small white flowers, solitary or in a branched inflorescence, consist of five short sepals, 3–5 mm (1/8–3/16 in.) long, and five white, slightly longer petals. These are deeply bi-lobed, a fact that often confuses amateurs, who think that it has 10 petals. The seed capsule opens by six teeth.

MERCKIA
Wilhelmsia physodes (Fisch.) McNeill
Syn. *Arenaria physodes* Fisch.
Syn. *Merckia physodes* (Fisch.) Cham. & Schlecht.

This is a creeping, prostrate plant with trailing stems up to 30 cm (12 in.) long. Paired, opposite, smooth leaves are small and oval, with a pointed tip. Small white-petalled flowers are solitary on short, silky-hairy stalks; the stamens are longer than the petals, the sepals and ovaries often reddish. This may be found on river gravel bars and moist sandy places throughout c. and n. Yukon, the Mackenzie delta, and most of Alas.

NYMPHAEACEAE Water Lily Family

YELLOW WATER LILY
Nuphar polysepala Engelm.

Large, showy, yellow flowers, up to 10 cm (4 in.) across, rise above the covering of lily pads. Most conspicuous are the 7–12 sepals, the four smallest outer ones being green, the remainder larger and bright yellow. Large, usually floating, heart-shaped leaves are connected to rhizomes on the muddy bottom by rounded petioles up to 2 m (6 ft.) long. The flowers brighten the surface of many ponds, shallow lakes and sluggish streams throughout the forested parts of the Yukon, n.w. BC and the Mackenzie valley. This species is found all over Alas. except in the extreme north. Another YELLOW WATER LILY, *N. variegata* Engelm., with smaller flowers and leaves, and flattened petioles, has been found in c. Yukon, which is the western limit of its range.

The rhizomes of yellow water lilies are an important year-long food source for beaver and muskrat and, in summer, moose.

RANUNCULACEAE
Crowfoot Family

NORTHERN MONKSHOOD
Aconitum delphiniifolium DC.
3–5 cm (1 3/16–2 in.) dark blue flowers, the upper sepal curiously hood-shaped, are borne in an open spike at the top of smooth, erect stems up to 1 m (3 ft.) tall. Leaves, borne on the stem, are few and deeply cleft, with five-lobed parts. This variable plant is quite common in moist subalpine meadows and thickets up to 1,550 m (5,100 ft.) from Alas. e. to the Richardson and Mackenzie Mtns., and in n. BC. All parts of the plant are extremely poisonous, especially the seeds and roots, which contain two highly toxic alkaloids, aconitine and aconine.

RED BANEBERRY
Actaea rubra (Ait.) Willd.
The smooth branched stems, up to 1 m (3 ft.) tall, bear two or three compound leaves over 30 cm (12 in.) long and two or three times thrice divided, the leaflets deeply saw-toothed. Above these are rounded clusters of small fuzzy white flowers. A magnifying glass is needed to distinguish the three to five sepals, five to ten slightly longer thread-like petals, and numerous stamens. Fruits are either brilliant red or white, oblong-ovoid in shape, and poisonous. This is a plant of open woodlands occurring through most of our area s. of the Arctic Circle.

SMALL-FLOWER ANEMONE
Anemone parviflora Michx.

From a firmly anchored, thick rootstock springs a tuft of much-divided, hairy-stalked leaves. One or two flower stems rise to 15 cm (6 in.), and are inter-rupted about mid-length by a ruff of leaves similar to but smaller than the basal leaves. Flowers, 3 cm (1 1/4 in.) wide, pure white or tinged with blue, give way to densely hairy fruiting heads. Flowering from mid-June onwards according to elevation, small-flower anemone may be found on dry rocky ledges and scree in s.w. Yukon and areas

of the Yukon River drainage system. It has also been reported from the Old Crow River and the Arctic coast, and the Mackenzie and Richardson Mtns. n. to the Mackenzie delta.

DRUMMOND'S ANEMONE
Anemone drummondii Wats.
Syn. *A. multiceps* (Greene) Standl.
Syn. *Pulsatilla multiceps* Greene

Drummond's anemone differs from the *A. parviflora* in that the stems are shorter, the sepals are deep purplish-blue on both sides (not white) and the anthers are almost black. Locally common in dry mats in calcareous soil and alpine tundra, it is found only in n. Alas. and the Yukon and in the Richardson Mtns.

CUT-LEAF ANEMONE
Anemone multifida Poir.
Many silky-haired stems up to 50 cm (20 in.) tall rise from a loosely tufted plant. Basal leaves are two or three times divided into narrowly lanceolate, acute lobes. Flower stems bear a collar of three leaves, also deeply divided. The solitary flowers have creamy-white or sometimes purplish sepals 5–10 mm (3/16–3/8 in.) long; they are followed by conspicuous, globose fruiting heads. This variable species, ranging from Alas. s., is common on roadsides and dry gravelly slopes over s. Yukon, n. BC, and the Mackenzie River drainage system.

NARCISSUS-FLOWERED ANEMONE
Anemone narcissiflora L.
This strikingly handsome and variable species is circumpolar in its many forms. It is usually more or less soft-hairy. In our area the flowers, in clusters of 2–5,

have six creamy-white sepals and are borne on stems not usually more than 20 cm (8 in.) high. Leaves on the flower stalk are deeply lobed, sessile and smaller than the long-petioled, ternately cleft basal ones. Lowland forms may be more robust, up to 60 cm (24 in.) tall. This is a plant of dry, rocky or grassy mountain slopes, flowering in early or late June according to location. It ranges through most of c. and s. Alas. and the Yukon, e. to the Richardson and Mackenzie Mtns., and n. almost to the Arctic coast.

PASQUE-FLOWER, WILD CROCUS, PRAIRIE CROCUS
Pulsatilla ludoviciana (Nutt.) Heller
Syn. *P. patens* (L.) Mill.
Syn. *Anemone patens* L.

A furry leaf cluster pushes upward through the cold wet ground soon after the

snow has melted. Unbranched stems, extending up to 50 cm (20 in.) tall after flowering, support the attractive purple flowers that open to as much as 8 cm (3 1/4 in.) in diameter. The flower stem has sessile leaves that are deeply cleft into linear lobes, as are the long-petioled basal leaves. These are formed in a rosette after flowering has finished. All parts of the plant except for the flower are covered in silky white hairs. The fruit, an achene, has a long feathery tail. A striking plant of open slopes and sandy, well-drained places throughout the Yukon and n.w. BC, it also ranges e. from n. and c. Alas. to Man., where it is the provincial emblem, and s. on the prairies to S. Dakota, of which it is the state flower. It was also the territorial flower of the Yukon, which has since been changed to fireweed.

YELLOW ANEMONE
Anemone richardsonii Hook.
Our only yellow anemone, this delicate plant is often mistaken for a buttercup. It has solitary stems, up to 10 cm (4 in.) tall, bearing single flowers and rising from a creeping rhizome. Leaves emerge along the rhizome, each one some distance from the next. They are three-lobed, the lobes shallowly divided and sharply toothed, as are the two or three sessile stem leaves. The showy flower has six bright yellow sepals; the fruit, an achene, has a distinctly long beak, recurved at the tip. Locally common in willow thickets, meadows and moist places up to over 1,400 m (4,500 ft.) and flowering by mid-June in some regions, yellow anemone ranges throughout our area. Like all the anemones this plant is highly poisonous.

BLUE COLUMBINE
Aquilegia brevistyla Hook.
Slender stems up to 1 m (3 ft.) tall (usually about 45 cm/1 1/2 ft.) rise from stout fibrous taproots. Basal leaves are long-petioled, trifoliate and much indented; those on the stem are sessile and smaller. The attractive nodding flowers, up to four per stem, have blue sepals and petals that are creamy white with pale bluish spurs. It is found on sunny, rocky slopes and open moist woodland in e. Alas., the southern part of the Yukon, n. BC and the Mackenzie River valley.

WESTERN COLUMBINE

Aquilegia formosa Fisch.

Fascinatingly lobed leaves almost suggest those of maidenhair ferns. The five coral-red sepals enhance the bright yellow of the flared tips of the five petals. These petals extend to a straight, orange-red spur. Stems may be up to 1 m (3 ft.) high, bearing three to six of the nodding, extremely graceful flowers. This beautiful plant is widely distributed. In our area it occurs in s.w. Yukon, south of 62° N.L. and in extreme n.w. BC, up to moderate elevations on mountain slopes, in open woodland or on gravel bars. It is more common in Skagway and Haines, Alas., and other coastal areas of the Alaska Panhandle out to the Kenai Peninsula.

MOUNTAIN MARSH MARIGOLD
Caltha leptosepala DC.

The bright green, fleshy leaves of this plant, with oblong wavy edges and long petioles, appear immediately after the snow melts, and are soon followed by the solitary (rarely in twos) 5–12-sepalled flowers. The sepals are narrow and creamy white, often bluish at the base. The flowers span about 4 cm (1 1/2 in.), and they soon drop sepals and clustered stamens to ripen a spreading cluster of follicles, each slightly hooked at the tip. In our area it is restricted to the mountains of n.w. BC and the adjacent Yukon, and in coastal Alas.

MARSH MARIGOLD, YELLOW MARSH MARIGOLD
Caltha palustris L.

This is a highly variable species, ranging in size from delicate arctic to coarse southern specimens. The long stem is often prostrate, the leaves reniform; the flower ranges from 1 cm (3/8 in.) in diameter in the Arctic to 3.5 cm (1 3/8 in.) in the more southern form. This has five yellow sepals and numerous clustered stamens, which are followed by a spreading cluster of follicles, each with a hooked beak. Ranging through Alas. into the c. and arctic coastal Yukon, the coarser form follows the coast from Alas. s. Marsh marigold contains a poison,

protoanemonin, which is broken down by boiling, according to Hultén's *Flora of Alaska*. A rarer species, FLOATING MARSH MARIGOLD, *C. natans* Pall., is an aquatic plant of mud and shallow ponds. It has a small white-sepalled flower bearing straight-beaked follicles in globular clusters, and ranges through c. Alas. and the Yukon.

TALL DELPHINIUM, TALL LARKSPUR
Delphinium glaucum Wats.

This stately plant, up to 2 m (6 ft.) or more tall, has dark, purple-blue flowers that are carried in a long spire that extends for about 30–45 cm (12–18 in.). Sepals are cupped forward, the upper one modified into a pronounced hollow spur 8–10 mm (3/8 in.) long. The numerous

leaves are glaucous and are reduced in size upward: they are deeply five- to seven-lobed, the lobes sharply toothed. It is found in subalpine and alpine meadows throughout our area and much of Alas. and in moist, wooded meadows and clearings at lower elevations. It is often fatal to cattle, which graze on it in the spring.

WATER CROWFOOT, WHITE WATER-BUTTERCUP
Ranunculus aquatilis L.

This aquatic buttercup has two kinds of leaves; those on the long submerged stems are divided into many thread-like branches, but the few floating on the surface are deeply cleft into three wide lobes. (The latter are not present in all forms.) Five thin sepals are soon shed, and the five unnotched petals are white, sometimes having a yellow base. The flowers give rise to a globular cluster of achenes. Found in shallow ponds and sluggish streams, it is circumboreal and occasional in the Yukon.

NORTHERN SEASIDE BUTTERCUP
Ranunculus cymbalaria Pursh

This is a low, tufted plant with trailing, strawberry-like runners that root freely at the nodes. The smooth, rather fleshy leaves are long-petioled; the blade, varying from ovate to kidney- or heart-shaped, is very variable in size and crenately toothed. The flowering stems, up to 20 cm (8 in.) tall, bear one to several flowers that are up to 1 cm (3/8 in.) in diameter with bright yellow petals, about the same length as the sepals. This is a plant of brackish ponds and muddy or wet sandy places. It is found from the Dawson area s., through s.w. and south-central Yukon, in the Mackenzie delta and in scattered locations through the NWT and Alas.

ESCHSCHOLTZ BUTTERCUP
Ranunculus eschscholtzii Schlecht.

The stems are smooth, rising 5–15 cm (2–6 in.) tall, from a basal cluster of leaves, and bear one to three stem leaves. These are three-cleft and again lobed, and they are uniform to oval in outline. The five sepals are usually smooth, though in some varieties covered with short yellow hairs, and somewhat reflexed before falling. The broad, overlapping petals are bright shiny yellow. This highly variable species is found on mountain slopes in most of the Yukon, s. Alas. and n.w. BC. It may be seen perched high on alpine exposures, or in thousands just below the melting snow on a soggy alpine meadow from late June to August.

YELLOW WATER CROWFOOT
Ranunculus gmelinii DC.

The creeping horizontal stems spread over mud or in shallow water in ponds, ditches or slow-moving streams. Tiny three-lobed cauline leaves, not more than 1 cm (3/8 in.) across, are again divided. The flowers, about 8 mm (5/16 in.) in diameter, are bright yellow, the petals longer than the sepals. The smooth achenes have a broad recurved beak. This little buttercup is found in the far north, c. Yukon and along the Canol Road. A larger form ranges farther s. in s.w. Yukon and through the Rockies. Another similar species, ARCTIC BUTTERCUP, *R. hyperboreus* Rottb., has much smaller 3–5-lobed leaves. It is common in shallow, fresh or brackish water, frequently growing amongst tall sedges and grasses by the edges of ponds. This species is circumpolar, occurring throughout most of our area.

SNOW BUTTERCUP
Ranunculus nivalis L.

These perennial plants have erect stems up to 30 cm (12 in.) tall, that bear solitary flowers with five yellow petals, longer than the hairy brown sepals. The many basal leaves, on petioles up to 10 cm (4 in.), have three to five lobes, which are again lobed or toothed. Two or three similarly shaped leaves are sessile. A circumpolar buttercup, it occurs in moist meadows and bogs in arctic and alpine tundra throughout our area. DWARF BUTTERCUP, *R. pygmaeus* Wahl., should also be mentioned here. This is a tiny, tufted, perennial plant bearing one or more slender, single-flowered stems. Basal leaves are deeply divided into three main lobes. Minute flowers have five yellow petals, 1–3 mm (1/16–1/8 in.) long, and five greenish petals about the same size. Found in moist, grassy meadows to at least 1,800 m (6,000 ft.), it is circumpolar and occurs throughout most of our area.

WESTERN BUTTERCUP

Ranunculus occidentalis Nutt. The plants average 30 cm (12 in.) in height, with leaves and stem either smooth or soft-pubescent. Basal leaves are deeply three-lobed, then again three- to four-lobed and toothed, but the alternate leaves of the stem are moderately dissected, the uppermost almost linear and entire. The five greenish sepals are sharply reflexed. Five to eight bright yellow petals are oblong, less than half as broad as long. The achenes have a slightly curved beak. This is a common species of moist, well-drained soil ranging from Alas. s. along the coast, but extending into s.w. Yukon. Another common buttercup of BC and s. Yukon is MACOUN'S BUTTERCUP, *R. macounii* Britt. The stems may be up to 1 m (3 ft.) tall or trailing, branching freely and rooting at the nodes. Leaves are long-petioled, the blade divided into three leaflets, deeply toothed and coarsely hirsute. Tiny yellow flowers are not more than 1 cm (3/8 in.) in diameter. This is a rather weedy species of roadsides and wet meadows.

CREEPING BUTTERCUP

Ranunculus repens L.

This invasive, though not unattractive, plant has been introduced into N. Amer. from Europe and has now moved into n.w. BC. It spreads in open places and roadside ditches by long, decumbent branches that root at the nodes. The creeping stem and long-petioled, three-foliate leaves, sometimes marked with white, are covered with short white hairs. Flowers, 2.5 cm (1 in.) wide, have soon-shed, greenish, hairy sepals and five to nine bright yellow petals, with wedge-shaped nectaries, centring many stamens and pistils. Another creeping species, CREEPING SPEARWORT, *R. reptans* L., is aptly named, for it pushes up a pair of 3–8 cm (1 1/4–3 1/8 in.)-long, spear-shaped leaves as well as a delicate flower stem 5–10 cm (2–4 in.) tall. This bears a solitary, bright yellow flower, about 5 mm (3/16 in.) in diameter. It ranges widely from Alas. on moist clay and sand shores e. across Canada, but not along the n. coast.

CURSED CROWFOOT, CELERY-LEAF CROWFOOT
Ranunculus sceleratus L.

This is an annual plant with an erect, much-branched stem up to 60 cm (24 in.) tall. The basal, long-petioled leaves are deeply three-parted and again divided. Small flowers have five yellow petals, 5–7 mm (1/4 in.) long, and five shorter, yellowish-green sepals, both reflexed and soon shed. Found in shallow ponds, mud flats and swamps through c. Alas., c. and s. Yukon, the upper Mackenzie River valley and n. BC, it is circumpolar in range. Cursed crowfoot is named for the high concentration of the poison protoanemonin, which it contains; if the leaves are rubbed against the skin, wounds may occur.

ARCTIC MEADOWRUE
Thalictrum alpinum L.

This small plant has compound basal leaves with dark green, fan-shaped leaflets. The usually leafless stem is up to 20 cm (8 in.) tall, with small, nodding, reddish-brown flowers that lack petals and have bright yellow anthers on long slender filaments (male plants), or whitish styles (female plants). It may be found in alpine meadows or on stony slopes throughout the Yukon, s. into n. BC, e. to the Mackenzie Mtns., and in the mountains of n. and s. Alas.

FEW-FLOWERED MEADOWRUE
Thalictrum sparsiflorum Turcz.

Tall slender stems, up to 1 m (3 ft.), have mostly stem leaves that are twice three-foliate, the leaflets round, toothed and thin. An open inflorescence bears few flowers (as the name implies) in nodding clusters, each with four pinkish-white sepals. This species has bisexual flowers (unlike some species that have separate male and female flowers) and is found in scattered locations in open meadows and thickets throughout Alas. and the Yukon except the extreme north. This is the showiest species of the genus *Thalictrum*. Another is VEINY MEADOWRUE, *T. venulosum* Trel., which has unisexual flowers on separate plants, and has basal as well as stem leaves. This is a prairie species found in the Mackenzie basin in our area, and around Dawson City, where it was possibly introduced.

PAPAVERACEAE Poppy Family

MACOUN'S POPPY
Papaver macounii Greene

Large yellow flowers are solitary on stems rarely more than 15 cm (6 in.) tall,

with long-petioled, five-pinnate, compound basal leaves. The capsule is narrowly obovoid or club-shaped, about 1 cm (3/8 in.) long and half as broad. This small, delicate, tufty plant is quite rare, ranging through n. and c. Alas. into n., c. and s.w. Yukon and e. to the Mackenzie River. It may be found in sandy or gravelly soil in mountains to over 1,400 m (4,500 ft.).

ICELAND POPPY
Papaver nudicaule L.

A loosely tufted plant with large yellow (less often white, red or orange) solitary flowers, nodding from the curved top of pubescent stems up to 50 cm (20 in.) tall. Leaves, often short-petioled, 4–20 cm (1 1/2–8 in.) long, are deeply pinnately cleft. Iceland poppy has been cultivated in Alas. and the Yukon and has escaped in several locations. It can be found by roadsides and in waste places through c. Alas. ranging to the Yukon around Dawson. This picture was taken near the Ogilvie River on the Dempster Hwy.

FUMARIACEAE Fumitory Family

YELLOW CORYDALIS, GOLDEN CORYDALIS
Corydalis aurea Willd.

A sprawling, much-branched plant, with many handsome, blue-green, thrice pinnately divided leaves. The flowers have bright golden corollas, each with an upper petal that is characteristically pouch-shaped. In June and early July the flowers give way to capsules about 2.5 cm (1 in.) long, which bear shiny black seeds. It is found in moist to well-drained places in open woods, thickets and roadside gravelly places from Alas. through s. Yukon and n. BC.

FEW-FLOWERED CORYDALIS
Corydalis pauciflora (Steph.) Pers.
Not only is this species usually "few flowered," but it is also tiny compared to the two other species of *Corydalis*. No more than 15–20 cm (6–8 in.) tall, the few leaves are less "feathery" than the other species, and the two to six flowers, in a terminal cluster, are bluish-violet to sky blue. White-flowered specimens have been found. This little alpine plant inhabits moist areas near and above timberline from Alas. and the Yukon e. to the Mackenzie Mtns. and s. to n. BC.

PALE CORYDALIS, ROCK HARLEQUIN
Corydalis sempervirens (L.) Pers.
The uniquely shaped, tubular flowers of *Corydalis* have four petals; the inner two are similar and joined at the tip, and one of the outer two is pouch-shaped at the base. In this species the pink petals are very distinctive, having vivid yellow tips. These flowers are borne three to six in racemes at the tips of a branched stem, and the capsules are erect when ripe (unlike other species). Leaves, stem and basal, may be up to three times pinnately compound. This is a rather weedy plant found in waste places and disturbed gravelly or rocky roadsides throughout the southern part of our area. It has been seen beside the Dempster Hwy as far n. as the NWT border.

BRASSICACEAE Mustard Family

WINTER CRESS
Barbarea orthoceras Ledeb.
This rather showy member of the Mustard Family has a single, stiff, ribbed stem up to 60 cm (24 in.) with numerous pinnately divided leaves that are moderately reduced upward. Similar basal leaves, up to 10 cm (4 in.) long, have much enlarged terminal lobes. From spring until July, clustered, small, bright yellow flowers are succeeded by long, straight, upright seed pods. A circumpolar plant, it may be found on stream banks and in moist places through most of our area, except in the far north. The young leaves have been eaten raw or boiled by some Native people.

LOW BRAYA
Braya humilis (C.A. Mey.) Robins.
This is a small, variable plant, often not more than 15 cm (6 in.) high. From a tuft of oblanceolate basal leaves rise branched or simple flowering stems bearing small flowers with white or lilac petals. The tight inflorescence elongates in fruit; mature siliques are 1–2 cm (3/8–3/4 in.) long. Often found on rather dry, rocky scree slopes (some forms preferring alluvial clay soils), this species ranges from n. and e. Alas., through the Yukon, n. BC, the Mackenzie River system and the Rockies in Alta.

ALPINE BITTERCRESS

Cardamine bellidifolia L.

A dwarf, tufted plant with a cluster of long-petioled, ovate leaves. Flowering stems, up to 10 cm (4 in.) high, bear two to five (or more) flowered inflorescences. Petals, about 3 mm (1/8 in.) long and milky white, are twice as long as the purple sepals. The erect siliques may be 2.5 cm (1 in.) long. This circumpolar species may be found in gravelly or mossy places below melting snow, along mountain streams or in shady rock crevices up to at least 1,800 m (6,000 ft.) throughout our area.

CUCKOO FLOWER

Cardamine pratensis L.

This is a perennial having a basal cluster of pinnately compound leaves with small, rounded, stalked leaflets. Those of the stem leaves are narrowly linear. Petals are white or rose-coloured with darker veins, three times the length of the sepals. The siliques, when mature, are 3–4 cm (1 3/8–1 5/8 in.) long with a short style. Cuckoo flower may be found in wet meadows, along creeks or in flood plains up to at least 450 m (1,500 ft.). A variable, circumboreal species, it is found throughout Alas., s. through the Yukon to the northernmost regions of BC and e. Its name must come from the cuckoo, the bird whose well-known call is heard throughout Eurasia.

PURPLE CRESS, BITTERCRESS
Cardamine purpurea Cham. & Schlecht.

This is a tufted plant with one to several flowering stems up to 10–15 cm (4–6 in.) tall, and numerous basal leaves. These are pinnately compound with one to three pairs of roundish leaflets and a broad, short, apical lobe. The few stem leaves are smaller. The flower has four petals (as do all species of the Mustard Family), which are purple (rarely white), the siliques 1–2 cm (3/8–3/4 in.) long. Found on wet hillsides or scree slopes up to 1,800 m (6,000 ft.), it ranges from c. Alas. to w. Yukon.

TANSY MUSTARD
Descurainia sophioides (Fisch.) O.E. Schultz

Up to 1 m (3 ft.) tall, the occasionally branched stem bears many pinnately compound leaves in the lower half; the leaves become single above. Tiny, greenish-yellow flowers at the tip of the spike are followed by erect 2.5 cm (1 in.)-long siliques. Found in gravel bars and disturbed places, it is widespread in our area, flowering through the summer months.

ALPINE DRABA
Draba alpina L.

This is a highly variable, small, tufted plant. It has many broad, lanceolate leaves with a prominent mid-rib and long, rather stiff hairs along the margins. The flowering stems, not more than about 15 cm (6 in.) high, are pubescent and leaf-less, and they bear short inflorescences of up to 10 flowers. The yellow petals are about twice as long as the hairy sepals. It is found in gravelly and rocky places in the mountains and on tundra. Circumpolar, it ranges through n. and e. Alas., the Mackenzie and Richardson Mtns., the n.w. coast of the Dist. of Mackenzie and in scattered locations in the mountains of c. and s.w. Yukon.

YELLOWSTONE DRABA
Draba incerta Payson

More than 30 species of *Draba* have been recorded in our area. Four are mentioned as a fair representation of the genus. The somewhat open tufts of this alpine perennial consist of short stems bearing numerous, partly overlapping, firm, linear-oblanceolate leaves, whose margins are crisp with short stiff hairs. The clusters of mustard-type flowers form yellow clumps on rocky slopes. The southern Yukon is about the northern limit of this species which, as the name

implies, ranges s. in the Rockies through Yellowstone Park. Another species, FEW-SEEDED DRABA, *D. oligosperma* Hook., has almost the same range and is very similar. In fact, the only major difference between the two is the length of the mature (or ripe) siliques, those of the few-seeded draba, up to 5 mm (3/16 in.) long, being half the length of those of the other species.

OGILVIE DRABA
Draba ogilviensis Hult.
Single, about 5 cm (2 in.) high, unbranched flowering stems, each with one or two pairs of smooth, deep green leaves, arise from the forks of long, trailing, branched, leafy stems. Petals, up to 6 mm (1/4 in.) long, are golden yellow. The inflorescence elongates in fruit, bearing oblong siliques up to 8 mm (5/16 in.) in length, with a slender 1 mm (1/32 in.) beak. This attractive little plant is known from the Mackenzie Mtns. of NWT, Ogilvie and St. Elias Mtns. in the Yukon and Alas., from about 1,100–1,900 m (3,600–6,300 ft.) in alpine meadows.

YELLOW WALLFLOWER
Erysimum angustatum Rydb.
This has a thick taproot with several upright stems and linear leaves. The four yellow, oblong-ovate petals have a claw (narrow base) about as long as the sepals. Siliques are linear and curved. This showy plant grows only in c. and w. Yukon, mostly around the Dawson area and adjacent Alas. The picture was taken near the western shore of Kluane Lake in a dry, disturbed gravelly area. This appears to be a relatively rare species.

PALLAS' WALLFLOWER
Erysimum pallasii (Pursh) Fern.
A rosette of linear-lanceolate leaves, 5–7 cm (2–2 3/4 in.) long, tapers gradually into a narrow petiole. The inflorescence is many-flowered, and when the first flowers expand, the flowering axis is so short that the flowers appear to develop at the base of the leaves; later the axis elongates to 15–35 cm (6–14 in.) long. The flowers are purple and fragrant. Siliques are long, up to 11 cm (4 1/2 in.), and curved. Inhabiting stony places on tundra, often near animal burrows or bird cliffs, it is circumpolar, found in the High Arctic and scattered throughout mountainous regions in our area.

ARCTIC BLADDERPOD
Lesquerella arctica (Wormskj.) S. Wats.
A small plant, it has flowering stems up to 20 cm (8 in.) tall arising from a clump of spatulate leaves. Yellow petals up to 7 mm (1/4 in.) long are about twice as long as the sepals. 7 mm (1/4 in.), erect, ovate siliques have 2 mm (1/16 in.) styles at the tips. Found on rocky hillsides and ridges in the mountains, it is widely scattered through much of Alas. and the Yukon, and e. *L. calderi* Mulligan & Porsild is considered a subspecies of *L. arctica* by some. It is distinguished by flowers up to 1 cm (3/8 in.) broad and larger siliques up to 8 mm (1/3 in).

PARRYA
Parrya nudicaulis (L.) Regel

This is a tufted plant with a cluster of oblanceolate basal leaves that are long-petioled, entire or slightly toothed, mostly smooth or slightly pubescent and somewhat fleshy. Flowering stems stand 10–20 cm or even 30 cm (4–12 in.) high when in fruit. The large, fragrant flowers have rose-purple or white petals 1.5 cm (5/8 in.) long. Siliques, 3–5 cm (1 1/4–2 in.) long, are wavy, with two to three large seeds in each locule. Parrya grows in moist, rather sandy places; it ranges throughout most of Alas., extending e. to the east slopes of the Mackenzie and Richardson Mtns. A highly variable species, it is found in a smaller form in the Arctic.

SMELOWSKIA
Smelowskia borealis (Greene) Drury & Rollins

Densely felted, grey-green leaves, 3–8 cm (1 1/4–3 1/4 in.) long (the cuneate blades narrowing to slender petioles and usually three-lobed in the apex) are borne in rosettes, the decumbent stems bearing smaller ones. Flowering takes place as the flowering heads appear among the basal leaves. Stems bear 20–40 flowers on 1 cm (3/8 in.)-long peduncles; these and the sepals are densely pubescent. Purple petals, 6 mm (1/4 in.) long, are about twice as long as the sepals. Siliques, 8–10 mm (3/8 in.) long, have one to three seeds in each locule. This attractive plant is found only in the unglaciated mountains of c. and n. Alas., w. Yukon and the n. Mackenzie Mtns.

DROSERACEAE Sundew Family

LONG-LEAVED SUNDEW

Drosera anglica Huds.

This plant may be seen sometimes in dense colonies, with rosettes of uniquely shaped leaves standing erect above the sphagnum moss. These long-petioled, narrowly spatulate leaves, three or four times longer than broad, are fringed with highly modified red hairs, each tipped with a drop of clear viscid fluid that is tinted ruby red. They are designed to attract and then ensnare crawling and flying insects by bending inwards. The insects' juices are then assimilated by digestive enzymes produced by the plant. A leafless, 15 cm (6 in.) flower stalk bears, at the top, a row of several white flowers along one side. These appear to open one at a time and only in bright sunshine. This species is widely distributed in N. Amer. and Eurasia; it has been found in several locations in the southern part of our area and in the Mackenzie River system in peat bogs.

ROUND-LEAVED SUNDEW

Drosera rotundifolia L.

The specific name refers to the roundish leaves, which, at the ends of long petioles, form a flat rosette partly hidden by the sphagnum and other mosses among which they grow. The leaf shape and habitat readily distinguish this from *D. anglica* (which see). The leaves of round-leaved sundew are also edged

with highly modified hairs, each tipped by a drop of sticky fluid. This is a trap for insects, which supplement the diet of the plant with phosphorus and nitrogen compounds, as these essential elements are not readily picked up by the roots from their watery and acid surroundings. The 5–20 mm (3/16–3/4 in.) leafless flower stalks bear small, four- to five-petalled, white flowers on one side at the top. This widespread circumboreal species ranges through the Yukon and the Mackenzie and Liard River drainage systems.

CRASSULACEAE
Stonecrop Family

LANCE-LEAVED STONECROP
Sedum lanceolatum Torr.

Plump leaves in a basal rosette, quite round in cross-section, vary in shape from linear to narrowly ovate. They are dark green, sometimes farinose, and generally become bronzed in late summer. From these basal leaves arise flowering stems about 20 cm (8 in.) tall with leaves spaced up their length. They bear pale yellow flowers in flattish heads. The five petals are sharp-pointed and separate to the base. This is found in rocky and dry sandy places through s. Yukon, most of BC, and s. in the Rockies. In the St. Elias Mtns. it ranges up to 1,800 m (6,000 ft.).

ROSEROOT
Sedum integrifolium (L.) A. Nels.
Syn. *Rhodiola rosea* L.

This plant has a thick, succulent, much-branched, scaly rhizome that emits the fragrance of roses when crushed or cut. This rhizome bears clusters of many leafy stems, 5–35 cm (2–14 in.) high. The leaves, alternate up the stem, are glaucous, and somewhat spoon-shaped, with variably dentate margins. Flowers are dense, in flattish to rounded clusters, and are often imperfect (having only vestigial stamens in the female flowers and abortive ovaries in the male flowers). They usually have purple or dark red (rarely yellow) petals, followed by plump, reddish follicles in the female flowers. Roseroot is locally common on scree slopes and rocky places in the mountains to at least 1,950 m (6,400 ft.) in our area. Succulent young stems and leaves are edible raw or cooked.

SAXIFRAGACEAE Saxifrage Family

ALASKA BOYKINIA, BEAR FLOWER
Boykinia richardsonii (Hook.) A. Gray
From a stout rhizome, densely covered in old leaf sheaths, arise a few conspicuous leaves. They are petioled, with uniform blades 5–10 cm (2–4 in.) in diameter, with dentate margins. The 30–50 cm (12–20 in.)-tall flowering stem, with a few small stem leaves, bears a congested spike of showy flowers. They have 1.5 cm (5/8 in.)-long, oblanceolate, white or pale pink petals. This showy plant grows only in the unglaciated mountains of n. and c. Alas. and n.w. Yukon. It may be found in subalpine meadows and thickets, along creek banks and on the edges of snow fields. It smells very strongly when bruised.

GOLDEN SAXIFRAGE
Chrysosplenium wrightii Franch. & Sav.
Small, yellowish-green perennial plants, up to 10 cm (4 in.) tall, grow from creeping rhizomes. The fleshy, alternate leaves are uniform and shallowly three- to seven-lobed, with thick petioles that are covered in rusty hairs. The small flowers have yellowish-green sepals with minute purple dots and eight stamens. Golden saxifrage is easily distinguished from the more widespread species, NORTHERN WATER-CARPET, *C. tetrandrum* (Lund) Fries, which has only four stamens, no rusty hairs on the petioles and no purple spots on the sepals. Found in moist alpine tundra, on river banks or in mud, it ranges from w. Alas. e. through the Yukon to the Richardson and Mackenzie Mtns.

LEATHER-LEAVED SAXIFRAGE, PEARLEAF

Leptarrhena pyrolifolia (D. Don) Ser. Compressed heads of small white flowers, each with 10 long stamens, are borne on a stem 15–40 cm (6–16 in.) tall that has one or two reduced leaves. This rises from a basal rosette of leathery leaves that are glossy green above, silvery green below. They are obovate, with pronounced teeth that point forward. The flowers are followed by showy reddish fruits. This is a plant of wet places, along creeks in the mountains up to at least 1,400 m (4,500 ft.), in coastal Alas. and throughout most of BC. It extends into s. Yukon and the Mackenzie Mtns.

STOLONIFEROUS MITREWORT

Mitella nuda L. A creeping rhizome gives rise to a cluster of long-petioled, cordate leaves with rounded-crenate margins. Usually leafless flower stems, about 15 cm (6 in.) long, rise from thin basal clusters, bearing a number of flowers, not more than 2 cm (3/4 in.) in diameter. The five, greenish-yellow, most unusually shaped petals look like branched threads, and the 10 stamens are inserted opposite to and alternate with them. This inconspicuous plant may be found in wet places in s. Yukon, extreme n. BC and along the Rockies. Another species, ALPINE MITREWORT, *M. pentandra* Hook., is more southerly in range and is found in s. Yukon. It is taller, with leaves that are more heart-shaped with unevenly dentate margins, and it has five stamens opposite each of the petals.

FRINGED GRASS-OF-PARNASSUS
Parnassia fimbriata Koenig

Basal leaves, rising from a short, perennial rootstock, spread their shiny, heart-shaped and entire blades at the end of smooth petioles 2 1/2–3 times as long. The 15–40 cm (6–16 in.) slender scapes have a clasping bract about halfway up and are terminated by a showy flower, about 2.5 cm (1 in.) in diameter. There are five elliptical sepals and five spreading, creamy-white petals, with five to seven conspicuous greenish veins, and they are fringed with fleshy hairs near the bases. This most attractive of the three species of *Parnassia* in our area may be found in wet meadows and on stream banks from southern and coastal Alas. through the southern part of the Yukon, and s. through BC and the Rockies; it flowers in early July in most locations.

KOTZEBUE GRASS-OF-PARNASSUS
Parnassia kotzebuei
Cham. & Schlecht.
Several slender, 6–20 cm (2 1/2–8 in.)-tall flower stems are leafless, or sometimes have a single leaf close to the base. These rise from a cluster of short-petioled, ovate-cordate, basal leaves. Calyx lobes have three to five veins and are 5–7 cm (2–2 3/4 in.) long, about the same length as, or slightly longer than, the elliptical white petals. A large ovoid capsule, twice as long as the calyx, is a conspicuous recognition feature of this species. It is often common in wet meadows, on lake shores or along creeks, in the mountains to at least 1,800 m (6,000 ft.). It ranges all through our area.

MARSH GRASS-OF-PARNASSUS, NORTHERN GRASS-OF-PARNASSUS, BOG STAR
Parnassia palustris L.
The slim, smooth flower stems, 10–25 cm (4–10 in.) tall, have a single bract less than halfway up, which is usually almost as large as the ovate to elliptical, short-petioled or nearly sessile, basal leaves. The five white petals, not fringed along their lower portions as in *P. fimbriata* Koenig (which see), are marked by a variable number of greenish veins. At the base of each petal are staminodia (modified, sterile stamens), each with 6–20 or more fingers, ending in a swollen knot. Staminodia are characteristic of the genus, and alternate with the five fertile stamens. This circumboreal species occurs along lake shores or in wet tundra from the Arctic throughout our area.

NORTHERN BLACK CURRANT

Ribes hudsonianum Richards.

Like all currant bushes, northern black currant is thornless; the gooseberries, on the other hand, are prickly. Stems with erect branches, up to 2 m (6 ft.) tall, have three-lobed, long-petioled leaves, the undersides of which are covered in fine hairs on the veins, and dotted with yellow glands. White flowers, in 8–10-flowered upright racemes, are strong-smelling. The berries are black and smooth, edible but bitter. Found in moist woodland and beside streams, this is a boreal species, ranging as far north as the treeline in our area. Another species, SKUNK CURRANT, *R. glandulosum* Grauer, has dark red, bristly berries that smell of skunk and have an unpleasant taste. It occurs in s. Alas., s. Yukon and n. BC.

SWAMP GOOSEBERRY, BRISTLY BLACK CURRANT, PRICKLY CURRANT

Ribes lacustre (Pers.) Poir.
This bristly shrub rarely reaches more than 1 m (3 ft.) high, with erect or spreading branches covered in prickles of two kinds: some are very numerous, short and slender; others are longer, stouter, and in groups of three and four where branchlets and leaf stipules arise. The 3–4 cm (1 1/2 in.)-broad leaves are three- to five-lobed, and further deeply toothed. Flowers are clustered in drooping racemes; they deepen from pinkish to cinnamon as they age, and are saucer-shaped. The purple-black, slightly hairy berries resemble domestic black currants, but the taste is more bitter. Swamp gooseberry may be found in moist, open woodland and on stream banks from s. Yukon through BC, c. Alas. and on the Kenai and Alaska Peninsula.

WILD GOOSEBERRY, NORTHERN GOOSEBERRY

Ribes oxyacanthoides L.
This is a low shrub with ascending or sometimes prostrate branches, rarely more than 50 cm (20 in.) tall (although known to grow to 1.5 m/5 ft.), bristly when young, with spines at the nodes. Leaves, three- to five-lobed, and 3–4 cm

(1 3/16–1 9/16 in.) broad, are pubescent underneath, and long-petioled. Flowers are borne in racemes of one to three. Petals and sepals are yellowish-green and tubular. Berries, about 1 cm (3/8 in.) in diameter, are purplish-black, smooth and edible. Wild gooseberry may be found in moist woods in the southern two-thirds of the Yukon, ranging e. and s. from there.

NORTHERN RED CURRANT, WILD RED CURRANT
Ribes triste Pall.

A shrub up to 1.5 m (4 1/2 ft.) tall, it has ascending or prostrate branches that may take root. Caudate leaves are three- to five-lobed, on long petioles, and pubescent. Purple flowers (6–15 per cluster) are borne on pubescent racemes. The ovoid berries are smooth, bright red and good to eat, though sour, and similar in taste to the garden red currant. It is found in wet meadows, woods and thickets throughout our area, easily identified by exfoliating bark.

WEDGE-LEAF SAXIFRAGE
Saxifraga adscendens L.

This small plant has a single stem not more than 10 cm (4 in.) high, which may be branched, and has small stem leaves. This rises from a dense rosette of basal leaves that are usually reddish or brownish in colour. They are, as the name implies, wedge-shaped, with the narrow end at the point of attachment, and usually with three to five teeth at the broad end. Small flowers have reddish-purple sepals, about half as long as the 3–6 mm (1/8–1/4 in.) white petals. It is found in rock crevices and moist, gravelly alpine situations in s. Yukon, where it is rare, c. Alas. and s. through BC and along the Rockies.

YELLOW MOUNTAIN SAXIFRAGE, GOLDEN SAXIFRAGE
Saxifraga aizoides L.

Entire, linear, sessile leaves end in an abrupt tip. Both basal and stem leaves appear smooth at first glance, but will be found to be covered with very small, pale, fleshy hairs. The 5–10 cm (2–4 in.) upright stems are leafy, and generally bear one golden-yellow flower, about 2 cm (3/4 in.) wide. A two-lobed pistil is typical of this family, but sometimes it is three-lobed. The 10 stamens have conspicuously large anthers, and the five, linear-long petals have narrow bases. The loose mats of light green, succulent leaves, partially hidden by masses of golden flowers may be found in stream banks, moist cliffs and talus slopes from e. Yukon, e. and s. through e. BC and Alta.

SPOTTED SAXIFRAGE, MATTED SAXIFRAGE
Saxifraga bronchialis L.

This beautiful perennial rock cover has evergreen leaves that are sufficiently variable to result in plants that appear quite unalike. They vary from harsh, slim-lanceolate and sharp-tipped, with rigid stubby hairs along the margins, to plants with much softer, thumb-shaped leaves with smaller, softer hairs. June–August, 5–15 cm (2–6 in.), much-branched flowering stems rise from the dense mat of leaves. Each branch is terminated by a round bud, which opens into a showy, 1.5 cm (5/8 in.) flower. The oval, white to cream petals are dotted with a series of round spots of pure spectrum tints, graduated from tip to base in crimson, through orange to chrome yellow. Found in rock crevices, and on cliffs, talus slopes and gravelly flats from tundra to woodlands, to at least 2,000 m (6,600 ft.) in the mountains, it is common in the unglaciated areas of the Yukon and Alas. s. to n.w. BC.

TUFTED SAXIFRAGE
Saxifraga cespitosa L.

The tuft of distinctive, finely glandular foliage identifies this 6–12 cm (2 1/2–4 3/4 in.)-tall plant. The leaves are tightly bundled in small whorls and are wedge-shaped, but with three-finger divisions at the tip. Two or three leaves, three-lobed like those of the basal rosette, alternate up the glandular scape, becoming entire upwards. There may be one to several white flowers up to 1.5 cm (5/8 in.) in diameter. The five ovate petals may be rounded, or slightly notched at the tip; the base is usually narrowed, and sometimes slightly clawed. This highly variable species is circumpolar, ranging through c. and s.w. Yukon and n.w. BC and the Arctic region of the NWT. It inhabits stony slopes, gravelly places, and tundra meadows and is found up to 2,000 m (6,600 ft.) in the St. Elias Mtns.

NODDING SAXIFRAGE, BULBLET SAXIFRAGE
Saxifraga cernua L.

Brownish-red bulblets in the axils of the stem leaves of the older stems make this saxifrage unmistakable. The basal and lower stem leaves are long-petioled and reniform (kidney-shaped) with five to seven lobes, the upper leaves much reduced. A single white flower, with 5–12 mm (3/16–1/2 in.) petals, about four times as long as the calyx lobes, tops each stem. This circumboreal species ranges along the Arctic coast of N. Amer., and also through c. Alas., c. and s.w. Yukon, n. BC, and s. along the Rockies. It may be found in arctic and alpine tundra, in moist places in the mountains, on cliffs and on scree slopes.

SLENDER SAXIFRAGE
Saxifraga radiata Small
This delicate plant bears white, egg-shaped bulblets at the base of the stems, which may be single or several and up to 20 cm (8 in.) high. The few basal leaves are long-petioled and have reniform blades shallowly five- to seven-lobed. Two to four flowers per stem have white petals with pale purple veins. This species inhabits moist alpine slopes and in our area it may be found in the Ogilvie, Richardson and Mackenzie Mtns.

SPIDER PLANT
Saxifraga flagellaris Willd.
A single, erect, leafy stem, up to 15 cm (6 in.) high, rises from a basal rosette of oblanceolate, acutely tipped leaves, whose margins are beset with coarse, spiny hairs. Also issuing from this rosette are a number of reddish, whip-like stolons, each terminating in a tiny, rooting rosette. The one to three large showy flowers have yellow, broadly ovate petals, two to three times as long as the sepals. Found in stony places, on scree slopes and on stream banks in the mountains to over 1,800 m (6,000 ft.), this variable species is circumpolar, ranging through the Yukon, the Richardson and Mackenzie Mtns., s. through BC and along the Rockies, and throughout s., e. and n. Alas.

STIFF-STEMMED SAXIFRAGE, RUSTY SAXIFRAGE

Saxifraga hieracifolia Waldst. & Kit.
This striking plant has sturdy, leafless, sometimes branched flower stems up to, and sometimes over, 50 cm (20 in.) tall. They rise from a basal rosette of oblong-lanceolate, usually smooth, petioled leaves, green above and often red underneath. Small flowers are borne in dense clusters in a spike-like raceme, each cluster subtended by a bract. The petals, no more than 3 mm (1/8 in.) long, are greenish-purple, about as long as the sepals. The flower clusters appear a rusty colour, hence the common name. This species may be found in alpine meadows through the s.w., c. and extreme n. regions of the Yukon, in the Mackenzie Mtns., and in the mountains of c. and n. Alas.

YELLOW MARSH SAXIFRAGE, BOG SAXIFRAGE

Saxifraga hirculus L.
Flowering stems up to 25 cm (10 in.) tall bear solitary (rarely more) flowers with bright yellow petals about 1 cm (3/8 in.) long, about twice as long as the hairy sepals. The stems rise from a tuft of numerous, lanceolate, petioled leaves from 1–3 cm (3/8–1 1/4 in.) long. The three or four linear stem leaves are sessile. A small and delicate plant of bogs and wet alpine meadows, it grows in most of Alas., except the s.e. and the extreme n., and in c. and s.w. Yukon, ranging e. through the Mackenzie and Richardson Mtns.

RED-STEMMED SAXIFRAGE
Saxifraga lyallii Engler

Red leafless flowering stems up to 40 cm (16 in.) tall rise from a long, dark brown rootstock, and a basal rosette of fan-shaped leaves. The leaves have many teeth, and taper abruptly into the petiole. The few flowers, 5–6 mm (1/4 in.) in diameter, are borne in an open panicle. The petals are white or reddish with two yellowish or greenish spots; the calyx is reflexed and purplish. Found in moist places in the mountains up to at least 1,100 m (3,600 ft.) it ranges from s. Alas., through c. Yukon, s. through BC, and e. to the Mackenzie Mtns.

HEART-LEAVED SAXIFRAGE
Saxifraga nelsoniana D. Don
Syn. *S. punctata* L.

Slender leafless flower stems up to 50 cm (20 in.) or more high terminate in a short raceme of tiny flowers. The petals, 2–3 mm (1/8 in.) long, are white to pink or rose and twice as long as the reflexed purplish sepals. The leaves, all basal, are more or less heart-shaped, on petioles at least twice as long as their diameter. They are distinctly dentate, ciliate in the margins, and may be pubescent or smooth. They are edible. This is a highly variable species that is found in its several forms throughout most of Alas., except the Yukon basin, extending e. through the Yukon to the Mackenzie and Richardson Mtns., past Great Bear Lake, to the n.e. Dist. of Mackenzie, and s.e. along the Rockies as far as Jasper. It grows in moist alpine meadows, on open hillsides and on stream banks.

PURPLE MOUNTAIN SAXIFRAGE, PURPLE SAXIFRAGE
Saxifraga oppositifolia L.

This very showy saxifrage is a low, matted plant, not more than 5 cm (2 in.) high; the tightly packed stem is dense with overlapping, opposite leaves in four rows. These leaves are 1–3.5 cm (3/8–1 3/8 in.) long, sessile, slim-pointed and entire. Their margins are fringed with stiff, rigid hairs, as are the margins of the five blunt lobes of the calyx. The attractively crimped, magenta or purple petals are accented by the brownish-orange anthers. A circumboreal plant, it occurs in tundra and alpine scree from Alas. throughout our area and s. through the Rockies.

YUKON SAXIFRAGE
Saxifraga reflexa Hook.

Rosettes of ovate, broad-petioled, rather leathery leaves that have dentate margins and are densely pubescent on both sides give rise to leafless flower stems. The two to three petals are white, 2–3 mm (1/8 in.) long, have a distinct single vein, and are nearly twice as long as the green (rarely purplish) reflexed sepals. The filaments are distinctly club-shaped. Found on tundra and dry, calcareous, rocky places throughout most of Alas. and the Yukon, it extends into the Mackenzie delta and the Richardson Mtns., and into extreme n.w. BC. Another species, ALPINE SAXIFRAGE, *S. nivalis* L., is very similar, but the leaves are smooth (not pubescent), the inflorescence is in denser clusters, the sepals are not reflexed and the filaments are not club-shaped. This prefers more acid conditions. Circumboreal, its range is much the same in our area as *S. reflexa*, but it extends into the Mackenzie and Rocky Mtns.

THYME-LEAVED SAXIFRAGE
Saxifraga serpyllifolia Pursh

This is a low, delicate, loosely tufted plant with trailing sterile and flowering shoots rising from perennial rosettes of smooth, rather fleshy, linear-oblong leaves, 5–10 mm (3/16–3/8 in.) long. Flowers are solitary on very slender stems, 2–5 cm (3/4–2 in.) long, with two or three bracts. Petals, bright yellow, are about 5 mm (3/16 in.) long, twice as long as the sepals. It is found on moist gravelly slopes or rock outcrops to at least 2,000 m (6,600 ft.) in the mountains in the far north, c. and s.w. Yukon and adjacent Alas., in extreme n.w. BC, and in the Mackenzie Mtns.

THREE-TOOTHED SAXIFRAGE, PRICKLY SAXIFRAGE
Saxifraga tricuspidata Rottb.

Large, densely matted cushions are usually formed. The leaves are reddish-tinged, rigid, leathery, spatulate or somewhat cuneate, with three pointed, tooth-like lobes at the apex. Flowering stems, up to 15 cm (6 in.) tall with a few alternate, reduced leaves terminate in inflorescences of usually many flowers. Elliptical petals, about 6 mm (1/4 in.) long, creamy white with yellow or orange spots near the base, are much longer than the sepals. This common saxifrage is found in dry, rocky and gravelly places in open or wooded areas to at least 1,800 m (6,000 ft.). It ranges throughout the whole of our area.

ROSACEAE Rose Family

SERVICEBERRY, SASKATOON BERRY
Amelanchier alnifolia (Nutt.) Nutt.

This shrub often reaches 4.5 m (15 ft.) in height, but in our area it is seldom more than 2 m (6 ft.), spreading underground and forming thickets. The reddish-brown branches become greyish with age. 2.5–5 cm (1–2 in.), simple, smooth leaves are alternate and deciduous. Short racemes of fragrant, showy, 2 cm (3/4 in.) flowers are white, rarely flushed with pink. The five-cleft calyx

withers, but is retained at the top of the mature fruit, which is a berry-like, purplish-black pome, like a tiny dark apple. The fruit contains a number of large hard seeds, which are spread by birds. It is juicy and sweet and may be eaten raw or cooked. A shrub of open woodland, in our area it is found along the Yukon River valley through c. and south–central Alas., in s. Yukon Territory, and in n. BC.

CHAMAERHODOS
Chamaerhodos erecta (L.) Bunge
A stout, woody taproot gives rise to a dense rosette of numerous, petioled, several times thrice-divided, hairy leaves. Many stems, up to 30 cm (12 in.) tall, and freely branched, have reduced leaves. The inflorescence is a many-flowered, much-branched, flat-topped cyme, making up about a quarter of the plant height. Small white flowers are rather inconspicuous; the petals, up to 3 mm (1/8 in.) long, are about the same length as the sepals. Smooth, pear-shaped achenes, 1.5 mm (1/16 in.) long, are greyish. It is found on dry, gravelly slopes or sandy flats and lake shores throughout s. Yukon and the upper Mackenzie basin, into n.w. BC.

YELLOW DRYAS, DRUMMOND'S MOUNTAIN AVENS
Dryas drummondii Richards.
The leaves are distinctive, very dark green above, contrasting with the strikingly white, densely haired lower surfaces. They are leathery, deeply crenate and almost glossy, and have edges that are crimped downward, especially in drought. At the top of each 10–25 cm (4–10 in.) scape is a nodding flower that never fully opens its 8–10 yellow petals. The calyx is densely covered with dark, glandular hairs. Flowers are followed by a ball of elongated plumy styles, each attached to an achene. Dense, low and extensive mats of this plant may be found covering gravel bars in rivers, lake shores and scree slopes. It extends through c. and s. Alas., c. and s. Yukon, n. BC and the upper Mackenzie basin, and s. through the Rockies.

MOUNTAIN AVENS, WHITE DRYAS

Dryas integrifolia M. Vahl

As the Latin name "integrifolia" (entire-leaved) implies, the leaves of this species have margins that are entire, or have a few teeth on the lower half. About three times as long as broad, they are lanceolate-oblong, distinctly broadest below the middle. Dark green, smooth and shiny above, they are white and woolly beneath. Hairy scapes, up to 2 cm (3/4 in.) high, arising from dense leaf mats, bear solitary flowers that expand to 2.5 cm (1 in.) in diameter. The petals are creamy white, the sepals narrow and acute. This species, like the others of the genus, has long, plumose styles on the fruit. Usually found in open rocky and gravelly areas and river flats, less common in tundra, it ranges throughout most of our area.

MOUNTAIN AVENS, EIGHT-PETALLED DRYAS

Dryas octopetala L.

This is very similar to the other species of white-flowered *Dryas* in our area, *D. integrifolia* (which see), with which it sometimes hybridizes. Unlike the latter, *D. octopetala* has leaf margins that are crenate-dentate for their entire length; also the leaves are wider, 2 1/2 times as long as broad, and the veins on the underside are more prominent with gland-tipped brown hairs and much-branched white hairs. Though the name indicates that there are eight petals per flower, seven- or nine-petalled flowers are occasionally encountered. Found in arctic and alpine tundra in the extreme n., c. and s.w. Yukon, in extreme n.w. BC and in the Mackenzie basin, eight-petalled dryas is the territorial flower of the NWT. *Dryas* species have adapted to the lack of nitrogen in their environment by developing root nodules that store this element, capturing it from the atmosphere.

WILD STRAWBERRY
Fragaria virginiana Duchesne

A single crown of long-petioled, compound leaves rises from a thick rhizome. Each leaf has three firm, cuneate-ovate, sharply toothed leaflets, silky beneath. Showy white flowers are borne in a few-flowered cyme. The juicy, red, tasty fruit is quite round with achenes sunk in pits in the surface. This is the common wild strawberry of the interior n.w., occurring in west-central and s.w. Yukon, in n. BC, and in the Mackenzie basin.

GLACIER AVENS
Geum glaciale Adams

A densely tufted plant, with pinnately compound basal leaves, it
has five to seven pairs of leaflets.
Leaves are smooth above, but
densely covered in soft, yellowish-
white hairs below, as are the petioles and the flowering stem. Large,
solitary flowers, 3–4 cm (1 1/2 in.)
in diameter, have five to eight
bright yellow, oval petals. Hairy
achenes have 2–3 cm (1 in.)-long
plumose styles. This showy *Geum*
of n. Alas. and the Yukon, and the
edge of the Mackenzie basin in the Richardson and Mackenzie Mtns. can be
found on rocky alpine slopes or dry heath, where flowers open soon after
snowmelt.

LARGE-LEAVED AVENS
Geum macrophyllum Willd.

"Macrophyllum" (large leaf) refers not to the whole leaf, but to the disproportionate size of the terminal leaflet which is reniform, shallowly five-lobed, and up to 8 cm (3 1/4 in.) in diameter, the other leaflets becoming progressively smaller downwards. These basal leaves, up to 30 cm (12 in.) long, rise from a stout rootstock. Stems, which may reach 1 m (3 ft.), are hairy on the lower half, and have a few short-petioled, three-lobed leaves below the inflorescence. Five bright yellow petals are backed by five small, pointed bractioles, alternating with five triangular, pointed calyx lobes. These soon reflex and
the petals open flat. The mass of yellow stamens drops early, exposing the developing ball-head of achenes. Occurring in damp thickets, meadows and open woodland, it ranges from Alas. through the middle and s. Yukon and n. BC.

ROSS' AVENS
Geum rossii (R. Br.) Ser.

A rosette of 6–10 cm (2 3/8–4 in.)-long, erect, smooth, pinnate leaves, bearing about seven pairs of cuneate leaflets, rises from a stout rootstock that is covered with the withered remains of old leaf bases. Flowering stems, one- or rarely two- or three-flowered, erect with a few reduced leaves, grow to 28 cm (11 in.) high. Large, showy flowers, 2–3 cm (1 in.) in diameter, have pale yellow, orbicular petals, longer than the sepals. The styles are not plumose. Found in moist alpine tundra and in dry stony places in much of Alas., it extends to the extreme n. and to c. Yukon.

PARTRIDGE FOOT

Luetkea pectinata (Pursh) Kuntze
This is easily mistaken at first for a member of the Saxifrage Family, but closer examination shows that instead of the stout, two-parted pistil and 5–10 stamens, there are four to six slender pistils and about 20 stamens, which place it firmly in the Rose Family. Crowded leaves forming basal tufts, and continuing alternately up the 10–12.5 cm (4–5 in.) flowering stems, are small, smooth, and three-parted on the outer extremity, then again three-toothed. Small white (occasionally cream or even very pale yellow) flowers are crowded in a short raceme. Masses of these flowers may partially hide the extensive velvety green mats of leaves on moist alpine slopes and stream banks. It occurs in s.e. Alas., in s. Yukon, and in n. BC. Luetke, after whom this plant is named, was a Russian sea captain in charge of the fourth Russian voyage around the world.

GLANDULAR CINQUEFOIL

Potentilla arguta Pursh
Stout erect stems, up to 1 m (3 ft.) high, together with tufted, basal, pinnate leaves, are generally glandular or viscid. Obovate leaflets are serrate, the terminal largest, the lower ones progressively smaller. Flowers are crowded in one large terminal cyme, or in several smaller lateral cymes. The petals, pale yellow or creamy white, are shorter or slightly longer than the sepals. It is found on dry rocky or gravelly slopes in south-central Alas., in the Dawson area and in s.w. Yukon.

TWO-FLOWERED CINQUEFOIL
Potentilla biflora Willd.

A densely tufted plant with basal leaves that are long-petioled, the fan-shaped blades having deep linear divisions with revolute margins, rises from a thick caudex. Stems up to 12 cm (4 3/4 in.) long bear, commonly, two flowers together that are about 1.5 cm (5/8 in.) in diameter. Bracts and sepals are triangular, and of about equal length. The petals, longer than the sepals, are pale yellow, and inverted heart-shaped. The receptacle is densely white-hairy. Found in tundra and alpine gravelly slopes up to 1,800 m (6,000 ft.) in the mountains, it ranges e. from the Brooks Range in Alas. to n. Yukon. It also extends e. from Denali National Park into w. Yukon, and from the eastern slopes of the Mackenzie Mtns. s. to the n.e. corner of BC.

MOUNTAIN MEADOW CINQUEFOIL
Potentilla diversifolia Lehm.

The leaves are very diverse, as the name implies. Generally, they are five- to seven-lobed, the lobes obovate in outline but deeply and rather sharply toothed.

In some forms the teeth extend almost to the mid-veins, so that a fernlike leaf is formed. Hairiness also is variable, from sparsely to densely sericeous. Leaflets are nearly always in the range of 1.5–3 cm (5/8–1 1/4 in.) long, either greenish or greyish above and below, but not whitish. Stems vary greatly in length, but may be up to 45 cm (18 in.) long, with numerous small flowers in an open cyme. The five yellow petals are usually twice as long as the lanceolate sepals, which are again about twice as long as the narrow bracts that alternate between the sepals. It occurs in moist alpine meadows and gravelly places in south-central Alas., in c. and s. Yukon and in n. BC.

PACIFIC SILVERWEED
Potentilla egedii Wormsk.
Some botanists regard this as a subspecies of *P. anserina* L. It is generally similar
to that species, but differs in its smaller size, glabrous stolons, and fewer leaflets
that are not silvery pubescent. This is a plant of sandy sea shores and river
banks; generally it is found along the Yukon River and the Pacific coast in Alas.,
in the s.w. Yukon, extreme n.e. BC and on the n. coast of the Dist. of Mackenzie.

ELEGANT CINQUEFOIL
Potentilla elegans Cham. & Schlecht.
A dwarf species, it forms dense round tufts of dark, reddish-brown leaf bases
and small, trifoliate basal leaves, the blades about 1 cm (3/8 in.) in diameter.

Stems bear single terminal flowers that barely overtop the
foliage. They are 6–8 mm (1/4
in.) in diameter, the petals pale
yellow to almost white. This is a
rare, high alpine plant of rocky
or gravelly places, found only in
a few locations in the mountainous areas of the Yukon, Alas.
and NWT.

SHRUBBY CINQUEFOIL
Potentilla fruticosa L.

This deciduous shrub forms a low, rounded bush, sometimes 1–1.5 m (3–4 1/2 ft.) high, which makes it easily recognizable within the genus *Potentilla*. Leaves are small and greyish-green, with a short, hairy petiole and three to five untoothed leaflets. The flowers are intensely yellow. Petals are broadly obovate, and almost imperceptibly notched. The achenes bear a short tuft of hair. This is a common plant in open and partly wooded muskeg or tundra n. of the tree limit. Generally, it is circumpolar with large gaps, ranging through most of Alas., and all of the Yukon, extreme n. BC and the Mackenzie basin.

SLENDER CINQUEFOIL
Potentilla gracilis Dougl.

This highly variable species can only be described here in general terms. From a cluster of basal leaves with long petioles arise one or several 40–80 cm (16–32 in.) stems, which are extensively branched upward, and bear usually one or two leaves without petioles. The basal leaves are palmate, with 3–11 "fingers." These lobes are very diverse in shape and degree of notching, and also (as is the entire plant) in kind and quantity of pubescence. The flowers, 2 cm (3/4 in.) or less in diameter, vary from pale to deeper yellow. Some plants are partially male-sterile, with notably small stamens. Stamens usually number 20. It is found in waste places and roadsides in the Yukon valley in c. and s.w. Yukon, extreme n.w. BC and south-central Alas.

HOOKER'S POTENTILLA
Potentilla hookeriana Lehm.

Clusters of grey-haired leaves, about 2.5 cm (1 in.) long, have three leaflets which are deeply toothed. They are densely clothed below with coarse, straight, greyish hairs and somewhat less densely above (so that the green of the actual leaf surface is visible). Bright yellow flowers are borne on scapes barely exceeding the leaf cluster in height. In other forms they may be erect, branched, up to 25 cm (10 in.) high and many-flowered. This very variable species is difficult to separate from the generally white-haired SNOW CINQUEFOIL, *P. nivea* L., which some botanists include as a subspecies of the former. There seems to be little doubt that hybridization has blended these two species in some areas. This plant, in its many forms, occurs in rocky and gravelly slopes, or in open woodland and tundra in most of our area.

ARCTIC CINQUEFOIL
Potentilla hyparctica Malte

Tufts of persistent brown stipules are hidden by trifoliate leaves on petioles 3–4 times as long as the blade. Flowering stems, 5–12 cm (2–4 1/2 in.) high, usually bear one to three flowers. These are about 1.5 cm (5/8 in.) in diameter, pale yellow, and inverted heart-shaped. It may be found on talus slopes, rocky places and alpine tundra in most of the mountains of Alas., most of the Yukon, the Mackenzie Mtns., n. BC and the Arctic coast e. of the Mackenzie delta.

MANY-CLEFT POTENTILLA
Potentilla multifida L.

Stems, often greenish-purple, vary from decumbent to erect, and are up to 30 cm (12 in.) tall, spreading from a stout, many-headed base. The basal leaves are nearly as long as the flowering stems; these are pinnately divided with five to seven leaflets, each dissected into narrow segments with revolute margins, dark green above and tomentose beneath. The stem leaves are similar but reduced. Flowers, small and numerous, are borne in leafy cymes. Yellow petals, nearly orbicular, are slightly longer than the sepals. It is found on lake shores, dry gravelly places and disturbed sites in open ground in s.e. Alas., w. Yukon, the Mackenzie River valley and around Great Slave Lake.

NORWEGIAN CINQUEFOIL
Potentilla norvegica L.

This annual, biennial or short-lived perennial, taprooted plant has an erect, sometimes branched stem that may reach 1 m (3 ft.). The leaves, mostly on the stem, have three leaflets, which are ovate to narrow-oblong and strongly serrate and hirsute. The inflorescence, a leafy cyme, has many small flowers. Petals, pale yellow, broadly ovate and retuse, are shorter than the hirsute, lanceolate, 4–6 mm (3/16 in.)-long sepals. Occurring in damp, open, waste ground and disturbed areas, this circumpolar species is common in our area.

SWAMP CINQUEFQIL

Potentilla palustris (L.) Scop.
This is a lush plant with long, smooth rhizomes that are submerged in bogs and marshes. They root at every node, and from these rise the erect aerial shoots, up to 1 m (3 ft.) high. These bear pinnately compound leaves, the five to seven leaflets being smooth and deeply toothed. The flowers of this *Potentilla* make its identification a simple matter. They are unusual, with long and conspicuous greenish-purple sepals, and much shorter, skimpy, pointed, wine-red petals. In wet meadows, marshes and in shallow water, this circumboreal species may be found throughout our area.

PENNSYLVANIA CINQUEFOIL

Potentilla pensylvanica L.
Erect, simple or branched stems, up to 75 cm (30 in.) tall, have three or four evenly spaced stem leaves. Basal leaves are pinnately compound; the five to nine leaflets, each divided deeply into linear oblong segments, have their upper surface green, the lower grey-tomentose. Stem leaves are similar, but reduced upward. The inflorescence is a rather compact, several-flowered, greyish-tomentose cyme. Bright yellow, obovate petals are about as long as the sepals. It is common in grassland, open forest and dry mountain slopes up to 1,100 m (3,600 ft.) in our area.

ONE–FLOWERED CINQUEFOIL
Potentilla uniflora Ledeb.
Syn. *P. ledebouriana* Pors.

Loose cushions of brown or blackened leaf remains are partially hidden by small, trifoliate leaves. The leaflets are broadly wedge-shaped or obovate, each with about seven large, regular teeth. Upper and lower leaf surfaces and the petioles are covered in a silky pubescence. Flowering stems, 5–25 cm (2–10 in.) tall, have one to three flowers, rarely more than 1.5 cm (5/8 in.) in diameter. The deep yellow obcordate petals fade to pale yellow. This highly variable species, which probably hybridizes with *P. villosula* (which see) and others, ranges through most of Alas. (except the Yukon River valley), extending e. to the Mackenzie River, s. through n. BC and along the Rockies.

HAIRY CINQUEFOIL
Potentilla villosula Yurtz.
Syn. *P. villosa* Pall.

A tufty plant with basal leaves that are palmately trifoliate, its leaflets are broad and ovate, coarsely toothed apically, and entire near the base. They are covered with silky hairs above, grey woolly hairs below, and are deeply veined. The leaf margins are outlined with silky hairs. Striking, 2.5 cm (1 in.)-wide, golden flowers are clustered low above the foliage. The petals are sharply notched and each bears an orange spot at the base. This is essentially a coastal species, extending inland from the White Pass area.

PRICKLY ROSE
Rosa acicularis Lindl.

A small shrub, sometimes reaching over 1 m (3 ft.) in height, it has pinnately compound leaves with three to seven opaque, serrate leaflets that are smooth above. The stem and branches are covered in bristles and slender prickles. Showy pink flowers are solitary, and 4–6 cm (1 1/2–2 3/8 in.) in diameter. The withered sepals are retained on the scarlet fruit. Ranging from Alas. e., it is very common throughout the Yukon, especially on roadsides and river banks, in clearings, open woods and meadows. The hips make good jam and jelly, and are rich in vitamin C.

DWARF RASPBERRY, NAGOON BERRY
Rubus arcticus L.
Syn. *R. acaulis* Michx.

This is a highly variable, dwarf, creeping shrub that pushes up stems 2.5–10 cm (1–4 in.) tall from perennial rhizomes. These bear two to five trifoliate leaves, the leaflets having dentate margins, and a single, attractive, deep pink or purple flower. Though the flowers are somewhat cupped, the petals, if pressed flat, will span 2.5 cm (1 in.) or more. The slim, pointed sepals are strongly reflexed. Toward the end of summer, dark red, palatable fruits appear that make excellent jam. Widely distributed in tundra and moist meadows and on stream banks, dwarf raspberry is locally common throughout our area. Another raspberry, WILD RASPBERRY, *R. idaeus* L., is common in much of our area except in the far north. This is an erect, woody shrub, up to 2 m (6 ft.) tall, with small white flowers and palatable red fruit that also makes excellent jam.

CLOUDBERRY

Rubus chamaemorus L.

A low, glabrous herb with erect flowering stems, up to 30 cm (12 in.) tall, but usually shorter, rises from a thin, creeping rootstock. The few leaves are round-reniform, leathery and shallowly five-lobed with serrated edges. Solitary flowers have white, obovate petals. The fruit, red at first, later turns yellow, becomes soft and juicy, and quickly drops off. It is very tasty and makes good jam. Circumpolar in distribution, cloudberry is common in peat bogs and moist open woodland throughout our area.

COMMON BURNET
Sanguisorba officinalis L.
This species is similar to *S. canadensis* (which see), but has broadly cylindrical flower spikes that are 1–2 cm (3/8–3/4 in.) long and purplish black. The basal leaves have 7–15 ovate to oblong leaflets and the stem has one or two reduced leaves. A circumpolar species of moist areas and river bars, it ranges through c. Alas., along the Yukon River and its tributaries in c. and n. Yukon, and has been found in the Mackenzie delta and along the Peel River.

SITKA BURNET
Sanguisorba canadensis L.
Syn. *S. sitchensis* C.A. Mey.
Syn. *S. stipulata* Raf.
This is a glabrous perennial plant up to 80 cm (32 in.) tall. The handsome, pinnately compound leaves are chiefly basal, as much as 30 cm (12 in.) long, with 9–17 leaflets. They are thin and smooth with a membranous stipule, rhombic-ovate in shape, and strikingly toothed along the margins. Flower stems, about 30–45 cm (12–18 in.) long, are smooth and sometimes branched above. The buds at the lower end of the long slim flower spikes open first, and then progress ring-like up the spike. These whitish to greenish flowers are sometimes purplish-tinged. Sitka burnet is a plant of swamps and moist meadows in s. and c. parts of the Yukon and Alas., ranging s. through BC.

SIBBALDIA
Sibbaldia procumbens L.

This is a low, matted plant, rising from a stout rootstock, with a rosette of basal leaves. These are ternately compound, each leaflet having three teeth at the tip, and white hair on both surfaces. The 1 cm (3/8 in.) flowers, on stems less than 10 cm (4 in.) high, have five minute, pale yellow, slim petals about half as long as the greenish calyx lobes. There

are only five stamens, an unusual feature in the Rose Family. It is found on mountain slopes and gravelly places where snow remains late, in the Mackenzie Mtns. and the Mackenzie delta, and from c. Yukon s.

WESTERN MOUNTAIN ASH, ROWAN TREE
Sorbus scopulina Greene

A rather variable, much-branched shrub, 1–3 m (3–10 ft.) high, occasionally forming thickets reaching 11 m (36 ft.). Leaves are pinnately compound with 11–15 oblong-lanceolate, glabrous and somewhat shiny leaflets. The small white fragrant flowers are numerous in dense, slightly rounded clusters, 8–15 cm (3–6 in.) across. The fruit is fleshy, berry-like, glossy and bright red. This species may be found on moist subalpine slopes of south-central Alas., and from c. Yukon and the upper Mackenzie basin s. Another somewhat shrubbier species, SITKA MOUNTAIN ASH, *S. sitchensis* Roem., has leaflets that are less pointed at the tip and have teeth limited to the upper half. It occurs in the Coast Mtns. in Alas., and may be found in extreme n.w. BC.

BEAUVERD'S SPIRAEA
Spiraea beauverdiana Schneid.
Syn. *S. stevenii* Rydb.
This is an erect shrub with branched, slender stems, usually about 50 cm (20 in.), but occasionally as much as 1 m (3 ft.) tall. The dark brown bark on older stems is continuously shed. Alternate leaves are oval, 1–2 cm (3/8–3/4 in.) long, pale beneath and glabrous, with shallowly crenate margins. The small white or pink-tinged flowers are crowded in 2–3 cm (1 in.) broad, flat-topped or hemispherical corymbs. The fruit is a dry capsule. This species occurs in muskeg, alpine meadows, and open woods throughout most of Alas., n. and c. Yukon, the Mackenzie Mtns. and the Mackenzie delta, and also in an area in the south between Carcross and the White Pass.

FABACEAE Pea Family

ALPINE MILK-VETCH, MOUNTAIN LOCOWEED
Astragalus alpinus L.
Stems, 5–20 cm (2–8 in.) tall, rising from perennial rootstocks, bear pinnate leaves, 5–15 cm (2–6 in.) long, whose 13–23 leaflets are greenish, but hairy and elliptical. The small flowers are pale to deep lilac, borne in crowded racemes. The hanging pods are brown and densely covered with black hairs. This circumpolar species occurs on grassy slopes, gravel and scree in the mountains up to 1,800 m (6,000 ft.) throughout our area; it is common in some regions of c. and s. Yukon, flowering in early to late June according to elevation. The name "locoweed" is derived from the fact that some species of *Astragalus* take up the element selenium, if it is present in large concentrations in the soil, and this often proves poisonous to grazing animals. There are at least 12 species of *Astragalus* found in our area, many of them appearing in s.w. Yukon and adjacent Alas., and a few ranging n. to the Arctic. The flower colours vary from white to yellow to lilac and purple. The four that are most likely to be encountered are illustrated, and others that may be of special interest are mentioned.

ARCTIC MILK-VETCH
Astragalus americanus (Hook.) M.E. Jones

Erect stems, reaching up to 1 m (3 ft.) tall from a woody perennial base, bear numerous, pinnately compound leaves 11–13 cm (4 3/8–5 1/8 in.) long. Leaflets, 3–4 cm (1 3/8 in.) long, are glabrous above, paler and sparsely hairy below. Oblong stipules at the bases of the leaves are 1–2 cm (5/8 in.) long. The flowers, 12–20 in short racemes, are yellowish-white, turning brown with age. Seed pods are about 2 cm (3/4 in.) long and smooth. This species occurs on gravelly or sandy soils, flood plains, lake shores and openings in thickets. From east-central Alas., through c. and s.w. Yukon, it extends across n. BC to the upper Mackenzie drainage system and s.

BODIN'S MILK-VETCH
Astragalus bodinii Sheld.

The only entirely prostrate, sprawling member of the Pea Family in our area, this species is easily recognizable. Its stems, up to 60 cm (24 in.) long, creep along the ground from a central taproot, forming dense mats with many pinnately compound leaves. These have up to 17 oblong to ovate leaflets not more than 1.5 cm (5/8 in.) long. Loose racemes bear up to 15 pink to purple flowers. The calyx has awl-shaped teeth and is covered with stiff black or white hairs. It is found in gravelly, sandy soils, on flood plains and roadsides, extending in range from c. Alas. into s.w. Yukon and extreme n.w. BC.

HAIRY ARCTIC MILK-VETCH
Astragalus umbellatus Bunge

This handsome milk-vetch has erect stems, 20–30 cm (8–12 in.) tall, that may be solitary or a few together, rising from a horizontal creeping rhizome. The pinnately compound leaves have 7–9 oblong leaflets, 2–2.5 cm (1 in.) long, dark green and glabrous above, sparsely white-hairy beneath. The calyx is cylindrical, greenish-yellow, drying to brown, the corolla deep yellow with white fringes. The legumes are black, hairy and hang down. Occurring in arctic and alpine tundra, stony slopes and subalpine meadows, it ranges e. from Alas. throughout the Yukon, and extreme n.e. BC.

An interesting little plant that may be encountered on gravel bars, flood plains or rocky outcrops in s.e. Alas., s.w. Yukon and adjacent BC is NUTZOTIN'S MILK-VETCH, *A. nutzotinensis* Rousseau. A small tufty plant with rather prostrate stems, the cream-coloured flowers, 2–4 per raceme, are suffused with pink. The smooth pod, 3–5 cm (1 1/8–2 in.) long, is curved into a semi-circle—a distinctive and unique feature of this species.

LIQUORICE-ROOT, BEAR ROOT
Hedysarum alpinum L.

Erect stems up to 60 cm (24 in.) tall rise from large, fleshy rhizomes. The pinnately compound leaves have 9–20 lanceolate leaflets and conspicuous brown stipules. Racemes, 3–15 cm (1 1/4–6 in.) long, occur on straight, 5–10 cm (2–4 in.) peduncles. There are 10–20 pink or pale purple (rarely white) flowers, 1.5–2 cm (3/4 in.) long, with the keel longer than the wings or banner. The genus *Hedysarum* is recognized by the unique, jointed shape of the seed pods, which are termed "loments." This boreal species ranges through most of Alas. and the whole of our area on rocky slopes, gravel bars and open forests. The roots are said to be edible and when cooked taste somewhat like young carrots, but care should be taken not to mistake this for *H. boreale* (which see), a similar species of much the same range, which is poisonous. *H. alpinum* roots are a favourite food of grizzly bears, which are experts at distinguishing them from the other species.

NORTHERN SWEET-VETCH, WILD SWEET PEA

Hedysarum boreale Nutt.

Syn. *H. mackenzii* Richards.

This species is quite similar to *H. alpinum* (which see), but differs in the following ways: the fewer leaflets, though smooth above, are covered in appressed silver hairs below; the stipules are inconspicuous and grey; the racemes are elongated on curved arching peduncles; the flowers are deep purple, larger than those of *H. alpinum*—up to 3 cm (1 1/4 in.) long—showy and sweet-scented; and the three to six loments in each legume are not net-veined—the veins are transverse. Wild sweet pea is found throughout our area on gravel river banks, lake shores and roadsides. It is important to distinguish between this poisonous species and *H. alpinum*, liquorice-root, which has tasty edible roots.

ARCTIC LUPINE

Lupinus arcticus Wats.

This tufted perennial plant has erect stems, up to 60 cm (24 in.) tall, and numerous palmately compound, long-petioled leaves. The elliptic-lanceolate, acute leaflets are bright green and smooth above, pubescent below. Dark blue, showy flowers, in tall racemes, are followed by pods 2–4 cm (3/4–1 1/2 in.) long, each containing 5–8 very poisonous seeds, covered with silky hairs. Arctic lupine occurs in moist tundra and on grassy alpine slopes throughout our area. Another species, NOOTKA LUPINE, *L. nootkatensis* Donn, occurs in our area in the extreme s.w. of the Yukon and throughout the coastal mountains of BC and Alas. One difference between the two is the leaves, those of the latter being shorter-petioled, the leaflets oblong-obovate to oblanceolate, less acute-tipped, and usually hairy on both sides. The two species hybridize readily where their ranges overlap.

SWEET CLOVER
Melilotus officinalis (L.) Lam.

Two species of sweet clover occur in our area. They are both tall, up to 2 m (6 ft.), much-branched, bushy perennials, with small flowers crowding a long, slender, tapering spike. The leaves are small and trifoliate, the leaflets 2.5–5 cm (1–2 in.) long. Small, one- or two-seeded pods are yellowish. *M. officinalis* has yellowish flowers; those of the other species, WHITE SWEET CLOVER, *M. albus* Desr., are white, and its leaves are narrower. These are not native plants. They have been introduced from Europe as cultivars and have reverted to the wild state, spreading far and wide, on roadsides and in waste places from c. Yukon s.

NORTHERN OXYTROPE
Oxytropis viscida Nutt.
Syn. *O. borealis* DC.
Syn. *O. glutinosa* Porsild

This is a small, tufted plant with pinnate leaves, bearing 16–25 (or more) oblong-ovate leaflets. These are distinctly clammy, owing to the presence of many microscopic glands, and when fresh they are fragrant. The tightly clustered raceme bears 5–10 bluish-purple flowers; the calyx is cylindrical and hairy with white and dark hairs. This is a species of calcareous screes, mountain slopes and sandy places, and grows only in the Arctic–alpine regions of e. Alas. and the adjacent Yukon, and the Mackenzie and Richardson Mtns., extending e. of the Mackenzie River delta on the n. coast.

LATE YELLOW LOCOWEED, NORTHERN YELLOW OXYTROPE, FIELD OXYTROPE

Oxytropis campestris (L.) DC.
Syn. *O. gracilis* (Nels.) Schum.

This is a tufty plant with basal, pinnately compound leaves up to 30 cm (12 in.) long, each with up to or more than 31 lanceolate leaflets that are densely silky-haired on both surfaces. Scapes, up to 30 cm (12 in.) high, bear many flowers in a dense spike. The flowers are yellow or occasionally white, and are sometimes tinged with purple. Oblong-ovate pods are 4 cm (1 1/2 in.) long with

both black and white hairs. Found in dry, sandy and gravelly places throughout our area and e. to the Mackenzie basin, it is common in s.w. Yukon. Late yellow locoweed is extremely toxic, as are most of the species of *Oxytropis* and *Astragalus* and it is a common cause of livestock poisoning. The name "locoweed" is derived from "locoism," a disease caused by poisoning from these plants, in which horses, cattle and sheep appear to be mentally disordered.

DEFLEXED OXYTROPE, PENDANT-POD CRAZYWEED

Oxytropis deflexa (Pall.) DC.

This variable species has many, more or less erect, compound leaves, each with up to 41 lanceolate leaflets not more than 2 cm (3/4 in.) long. The leaves are often basal, but there may be a short decumbent, leafy stem. Few-flowered racemes stand well above the leaves, the petals varying in colour from whitish to bluish to pink-purple. The seed pods are pendant. This attractive plant of moist meadows, river banks and open woodland occurs in a variety of forms from extreme n. and s.e. Alas., e. through c. and s.w. Yukon into extreme n.w. BC, s.w. through the Rockies, and in the Mackenzie River delta.

JORDAL'S OXYTROPE

Oxytropis jordalii Porsild
Very similar to *O. campestris* (which see), under which some would give it subspecies status, this is a smaller plant with distinct features. The leaves are barely 6 cm (2 3/8 in.) long with 9–11 narrowly lanceolate leaflets, smooth above and silvery-hairy beneath. Flower stalks, up to 14 cm (5 1/2 in.) tall, are dark purplish, with 3–5 flowers. The 1 cm (3/8 in.) corolla is pale greenish-yellow, drying to ivory white. It grows only on the dry tundra in n. Alas. and the Yukon, and in the Mackenzie and Richardson Mtns.

MAYDELL'S OXYTROPE

Oxytropis maydelliana Trautv.
This tufty plant has a branching caudex covered with dark, reddish-brown stipules that remain attached. Pinnate leaves with greenish stipules, aging reddish-brown, have 11–21 ovate to lanceolate leaflets that are covered in straight, soft hairs. Hairy scapes bear many-flowered racemes in dense clusters. The yellow-petalled flowers are followed by ovoid pods, each with a long bent beak. An Arctic species, it occurs n. of the Arctic Circle, and throughout w. Yukon with scattered locations on the east slopes of the Mackenzie and Richardson Mtns.

SHOWY CRAZYWEED, SHOWY LOCOWEED

Oxytropis splendens Dougl.

Attractive silky leaves form a dense cluster up to 2.5 cm (1 in.) high. The numerous leaflets are arranged in whorls of three to six. They are pointed-elliptical, from 1–2.5 cm (3/8–1 in.) long. The flower stalks generally lengthen to hold the dense purple spike slightly above the mass of silvery foliage. The calyx is silky-haired and is about two-thirds the length of the rose-purple corolla, which has a standard slightly longer than the wings and keel. The pod is slim-pointed, and about 1.5 cm (5/8 in.) long. Found on dry, sandy, shady and grassy slopes, showy crazyweed ranges from eastern Alas., through the Yukon River valley, s.e. along the east slope of the Rockies.

BLACKISH CRAZYWEED

Oxytropis nigrescens (Pall.) Fisch.

A densely tufted plant rises from a taproot and branching caudex, covered with dried stipules and petioles that remain attached. Pinnate leaves have 7–15 linear-elliptical leaflets, less than 1 cm (3/8 in.) long and hirsute. An erect flower stalk, 4 cm (1 1/2 in.) long, bears racemes with only one or two spreading flowers that are bright purple, occasionally whitish. The calyx is shaggy-hirsute with black hairs. The standard has a blade that is obcordate. The oblong-ellipsoid pods are less than 3.5 cm (1 3/8 in.) long. Blackish crazyweed occurs in tundra and on rocky slopes throughout the Yukon, up to at least 1,650 m (5,400 ft.), and in BC n. of 59° N.L.

GERANIACEAE Geranium Family

CRANESBILL, WILD GERANIUM, NORTHERN GERANIUM

Geranium erianthum DC.

A perennial plant, its erect stems, up to 80 cm (32 in.) tall, rise from a thick rhizome. Both basal and lower stem leaves have long petioles; the upper are sessile. The leaves are three to five times deeply cleft, nearly to the base, with narrow, irregular incisions; three to five, or more, flowers barely top the leaves. Sepals are half the length of the rose, violet or (rarely) white petals, which may be up to 2 cm (3/4 in.) long. The thin, pointed fruit, about 1 cm (3/8 in.) long, resembles the bill of a crane or stork, before it splits into separate one-seeded segments. Occurring in forests, thickets, tundra, meadows and on roadsides near the s.w. border of the Yukon, and n.w. BC, it ranges through s. Alas. and s. along the Coast Mtns. Two other species of geranium found in our area are not illustrated here. WHITE GERANIUM, *G. richardsonii* Fisch. and Trautv., occurring c. and s.e. Yukon, has large white or purplish petals with purplish veins, and long white hairs on the inside to about half their length; BICKNELL'S GERANIUM, *G. bicknellii* Britt., has smaller leaves and many smaller flowers per plant, the pale purple petals only slightly longer than the sepals. This may be found in west-central and s. Yukon and n. BC.

LINACEAE Flax Family

WILD FLAX

Linum lewisii Pursh

Syn. *L. perenne* L.

Tall, very slender, smooth stems are alternately leafy with grey-green, linear, and entire 2.5 cm (1 in.)-long leaves. They bear flowers that have five lanceolate and membranous-edged sepals and five deep blue, delicate petals, 1.5–2.5 cm (5/8–1 in.) long, that are soon dropped. The shining brown seed capsules, about 6 mm (1/4 in.) across, contain many seeds that are rich in oil. (Commercial linseed oil comes from another species of *Linum*.) Widely distributed through w. N. Amer., wild flax may be found through much of our area in dry, rocky or gravelly places.

EMPETRACEAE
Crowberry Family

CROWBERRY
Empetrum nigrum L.

This low, creeping plant has 3–8 mm (1/8–5/16 in.)-long leaves that are dark green and linear, resembling tiny fat fir needles, deeply grooved beneath. They are arranged chiefly in whorls of four along the tough, prostrate stems. Tiny, obscure, solitary, dark purple flowers, lacking petals, are borne in the leaf axils. They are followed by the distinctive shiny black fruit. It may be found in very acid conditions in bogs and moist places amongst sphagnum and other mosses. It is circumboreal, ranging through our area, and is common in the far north where the berries are an important food source to the Inuit. They are juicy and sweet, but the seeds can be bitter.

VIOLACEAE Violet Family

WESTERN DOG-VIOLET
Viola adunca Sm.

A highly variable species, its leaves are most frequently heart-shaped, but may be ovate or obtuse, and are finely crenate. Some plants are smooth, others are densely hairy. Flowers are pale blue to deep violet, the three lower petals whitish at their bases, and they have purple lines that probably serve as honey guides. The lateral pair of lower petals is bearded with long, white, stiff hairs near the inner end; the style is also bearded near the tip. Found in dry meadows and forests, this species ranges from s. Yukon s. and e.

MARSH VIOLET
Viola epipsila Ledeb.
This is a small plant with thin, creeping rhizomes, and sometimes thread-like, leafy stolons. Delicate, smooth, heart-shaped leaves, slightly crenate, arise from the rhizomes on long petioles. The long thin peduncle, smooth, with a pair of bracts above the middle, bears one or two flowers. Sepals are oblong-ovate and blunt, the petals violet to lilac, the lower with dark veins. Occurring in wet meadows and bogs and on stream banks, to 1,650 m (5,400 ft.) in the mountains, marsh violet ranges through Alas. and the Yukon, extending s. through BC and e. through the Mackenzie Mtns. to Great Slave Lake.

ALASKA VIOLET
Viola langsdorfii Fisch.
The heart-shaped leaves are about 5 cm (2 in.) long; the basal leaves have petioles as long as 20 cm (8 in.), but the stem leaves have only short petioles. The flowers are pale violet, the petals usually flushed with white but yellow at their bases. The three lower petals are darkly lined, the two lateral petals white-bearded in their lower part. This is essentially a coastal species of bogs and wet forests, its range stretching from the Aleutian Is. and s. Alas., down the Pacific coast. It grows in the White Pass and Lake Bennett region and has been located in the Mayo district and the McArthur Range, but is considered rare in the interior of the Yukon.

ELAEAGNACEAE Oleaster Family

SILVERBERRY
Elaeagnus commutata Bernh.

A handsome shrub, 2 m (6 ft.) tall, whose greyish-red branches are hung in the spring with striking silver leaves, 2.5–7.5 cm (1–3 in.) long, pointed-oval, and entire-margined. From the axils of the leaves, almost stemless, cone-shaped flowers appear in twos and threes, June–July. These are quite unique: silvery on the outside and yellow within, with a pleasant perfume. The four lobes of the tubular calyx are flared outwards. There are no petals, but four stamens grow from the calyx tube around a short style. The fruit is silvery and obovate, dry and mealy and, according to Hultén, eaten, cooked in moose fat, by First Nations. Often forming patches several metres in diameter, this shrub can be found on dry slopes and gravel bars and in open spaces and aspen woods up to 1,100 m (3,600 ft.). It ranges through c. Alas. into c. and s. Yukon, and from the Peel and Mackenzie basins e. and s.

SOOPOLALLIE, BUFFALO-BERRY, SOAPBERRY
Shepherdia canadensis (L.) Nutt.

An open shrub that may reach 1.5 m (5 ft.) in height, it is easily recognized at any time of year by its orange-dotted white bark that gives the branches a rusty appearance. The thick, leathery, 6 cm (2 1/2 in.)-long opposite leaves are elliptical-ovate, with entire margins. They have silver stellate hairs and brown scurfy scales on the lower surface, and stellate hairs on the upper dark green surface. Tiny, reddish, clustered flowers appear in early spring before the leaves. They are of two kinds, male and female, borne on separate shrubs. The fruits are bright red and shiny, juicy but bitter, due to the presence of the glucoside saponin. However, some First Nations beat them in water to produce a thick foamy liquid that makes a refreshing drink. It occurs in open woods, thickets and gravel bars from e. Alas. throughout our area.

ONAGRACEAE
Evening Primrose Family

ENCHANTER'S NIGHTSHADE
Circaea alpina L.

A delicate plant, up to 15 cm (6 in.) tall, it grows from a tuberous rhizome. Opposite, long-petioled, ovate to sub-cordate, pale green leaves have shallowly dentate margins. The tiny flowers are borne in terminal racemes, each with two calyx lobes, and the two petals, lobed to about the middle, are white or pink. The 2 mm (1/16 in.)-long fruit is covered in hooked bristles. This is an insignificant-appearing plant of deep woods that occurs near the Yukon–BC border in the upper Liard River valley, coastal and interior Alas., and in extreme n.w. BC.

SWAMP WILLOW-HERB
Epilobium palustre L.

This delicate willow-herb has a single, slender stem 10–40 cm (4–16 in.) high, stiffly erect with thread-like stolons issuing from the base. Leaves, opposite (at least below), are oblong-ovate, 1.5–5 cm (5/8–2 in.) long and glabrous. The flowers, small and drooping when young, with pink or white petals, are followed by pubescent capsules 2.5–3.5 cm (1–1 3/8 in.) long. Occurring on river banks, in moist meadows and in wet places, this species is circumboreal, ranging through Alas. and across Canada; it is found throughout our area. There are at least six other species of *Epilobium* that are found occasionally in our area.

FIREWEED, WILLOW-HERB
Epilobium angustifolium L.

Unbranched, erect stems, often 2 m (6 ft.)
(occasionally up to 3 m/9 ft.) tall, bear
smooth, lanceolate leaves to the summit.
Racemes begin to flower at the base, and
become greatly elongated during the long
flowering season—July–Sept. in our area.
Commonly, the flowers are rose pink but
specimens with white petals and sepals, white
petals and red sepals, or pink petals and dark
red sepals may occasionally be found in parts
of the Yukon. Seeds are covered in fluffy hair
and carried great distances by the wind. One
of the most attractive plants of the north, this
is the territorial flower of the Yukon. It often
covers extensive areas on roadsides, meadows,
forests, river bars and burned-over areas.
Circumboreal, it ranges throughout our area.
All parts of the plant are edible.

BROAD-LEAVED FIREWEED, DWARF FIREWEED, RIVER BEAUTY
Epilobium latifolium L.

This is a low, bushy plant with clustered stems 10–40 cm (4–16 in.) tall. They bear somewhat waxy, bluish-green lanceolate leaves, carried in pairs that are opposite (at least below). These are variably entire to slightly toothed, and increase in length upward to about 6 cm (2 3/8 in.). The four slim, pointed sepals are purplish, and the four obovate petals rose to pale purple (occasionally white). The tuft of hairs topping each seed is buff-coloured. Large natural beds of this plant often occur in river bars, along roadsides and to 1,800 m (6,000 ft.) in the mountains, making a blaze of colour, July–Aug. It ranges through Alas. and the Yukon, across n. Canada and s. through BC. According to Porsild and Cody, the flowers may be eaten raw as a salad, and the fleshy leaves are edible when cooked.

APIACEAE Parsnip Family

THOROUGH-WORT, THOROUGHWAX

Bupleurum americanum Coult & Rose
Syn. *B. triradiatum* Adams

Smooth stems, up to 50 cm (20 in.) tall, rise from a short branching base. The basal leaves are linear-lanceolate, those of the stem usually broader and somewhat clasping. Umbels of two to nine rays are compact with tiny flowers, having bractlets and petals that are bright yellow. These are followed by brown, oblong, flattened fruit, 3 mm (1/8 in.) long with slender ribs. Thorough-wort can be recognized instantly within this family by its bright yellow flowers and simple, linear leaves. Found in gravelly or sandy places on river banks and on talus slopes, it ranges through c. and n. Alas., into w. Yukon, and e. to the Mackenzie delta.

NORTHERN HEMLOCK-PARSLEY

Sium suave Walt.

Robust, smooth, simple or branched stems, up to 60 cm (24 in.) or more tall, have long-petioled lower leaves; these are doubly pinnate-pinnatifid, the upper ones nearly sessile. The umbels have numerous rays with white or purplish flowers that are followed by ovate, 5 mm (5/16 in.)-long fruits. It is found on sandy river banks and gravel bars in the extreme s. of the Yukon and coastal Alas. Another member of this family, MACKENZIE'S WATER-HEMLOCK, *Cicuta virosa* L. is a robust plant up to 1 m (3 ft.) tall. It grows from tuberous-thickened and chambered roots that contain cicutotoxin, a deadly poison. Leaves are once or twice pinnately compound and the white to cream or pink flowers are in umbels with 14–33 unequal rays. It occurs in marshes, on lake margins or along streams in s.w. and c. Alas., c. Yukon and e. to Great Slave Lake, sometimes growing in water 50 cm (20 in.) deep.

COW PARSNIP

Heracleum maximum Bartr.
Syn. *H. lanatum* Michx.

A robust perennial plant, it has thick, hollow, much-branched stems from a single basal shoot that may reach as much as 2 m (6 ft.) high. Stems and leaves are usually woolly-haired. Leaves spring from a large sheathing petiole that has three large leaflets, each of which may be 15 cm (6 in.) long. These are coarsely toothed and palmately lobed, their size making the plant easily recognizable. The flattened compound umbel is often 20–25 cm (8–10 in.) across; it is made up of small flowers, usually greenish-white, occasionally yellowish or even pinkish. The fruits are pleasantly aromatic. They are much flattened, ribbed, and marked by easily visible oil tubes that extend downward from the tip. Cow parsnip is a widespread plant of stream banks and moist low ground from c. Alas. and c. Yukon e. and s. The stems have been used as a food source by First Nations. However, unless one is positive of one's identification, it is dangerous to try eating the plant; some members of this family, notably *Cicuta virosa* (which see) contain deadly poisons.

CORNACEAE Dogwood Family

RED OSIER DOGWOOD, WESTERN DOGWOOD

Cornus stolonifera Michx.

When the leaves have fallen in winter, the bright red stems, often in dense thickets up to 3.5 m (12 ft.) high, are most conspicuous. The heavily veined, ovate-elliptical opposite leaves, paler beneath, turn a showy plum colour in late summer. Flat-topped clusters of greenish-white flowers appear May–July. Each has

four small sepals and four spreading, pointed-oval petals, with stamens, placed flat between them, and a single, club-shaped pistil. The cluster of bluish-white drupes contrasts with the brilliantly coloured leaves and stems in the fall. A widespread shrub of wet swampy places and moist woods, thickets and clearings, it ranges from c. Alas. through the Yukon and Mackenzie River valleys and s. through BC. It reaches north of 65° N.L. only in the Mackenzie delta and the Peel drainage system.

DWARF DOGWOOD, BUNCHBERRY

Cornus canadensis L.

This captivating plant is seldom more than 20 cm (8 in.) tall, spreading by creeping rootstock to carpet the forest floor. The name bunchberry refers to the bright red "berries" that are borne in handsome clusters in the fall. In August they replace the numerous tiny "true" flowers, in tight clusters, that form the close-packed centre of the flower head from early June. These flower clusters are surrounded by four (occasionally three to seven) 2 cm (3/4 in.)-long, ovate, cream-coloured bracts which are, in fact, modified leaves. The four to seven elliptical green leaves form a whorl beneath the inflorescence. In the fall these become bronze and purple foils to the vermillion fruit. Carpets of dwarf dogwood occur quite commonly in clearings and in moist forests through Alas. and throughout our area, except in the far north.

PYROLACEAE Wintergreen Family

SINGLE DELIGHT
Moneses uniflora (L.) Gray

This delicate plant, from a thin, creeping rhizome, has a single bloom hanging from the top of a slender stem about 10 cm (4 in.) tall. Basal leaves are evergreen, roundish, and 2 cm (3/4 in.) long, with margins variably serrate to almost entire; the petioles are one-half to nearly as long as the blades. Triangular, waxen-white petals are held flat or slightly reflexed. The five pairs of stamens accent the salverform, 2 cm (3/4 in.)-wide flower. In the centre, rising from a large, green, five-grooved ovary, is a straight pistil, its summit sharply expanded and then divided into five upward-pointing, triangular teeth. Single delight occurs in moist mossy forests from Alas. across Canada, and throughout our area to at least 1,800 m (6,000 ft.) in the mountains.

LARGE WINTERGREEN, PINK-FLOWERED WINTERGREEN

Pyrola asarifolia Michx.

This handsome plant has a basal rosette of thick, roundish to elliptical leaves, about 4–8 cm (1 1/2–3 in.) long, with petioles at least as long as the blade. They are leathery, glossy, dark green above and often purplish below, with edges slightly wavy to sparsely and minutely toothed. The pink flowers, each with its strongly curved and prominent style, are about 1.5 cm (5/8 in.) wide. There are five sepals, joined at their bases, five separate petals, thick, waxy and elliptical, and 10 stamens. This is a widespread species of damp, open, mossy forests and stream banks, sometimes to considerable altitudes, throughout our area and Alas., except in the extreme north.

GREENISH-FLOWERED WINTERGREEN
Pyrola chlorantha Sw.
Syn. *P. virens* Schweigg

This plant is similar in some features to *Orthilia secunda* (which see) but the greenish flowers are all around the stem, not just on one side. The leaves are basal. They are few and long-petioled, with a small blade, which is yellowish green, shiny and somewhat crenate. 10–20 cm (4–8 in.)-tall stems bear open racemes of small flowers with greenish-white petals. The style is strongly curved with a distinct collar below the stigma, which has five knobs on its upper surface. The anthers are yellow. This is a common species of woods and thickets in s. e. Alas., c. and s. Yukon, the Mackenzie River valley and throughout n. BC. A similar species, LESSER WINTERGREEN, *P. minor* L., has rather oblong, dark green, dull leaves with petioles often longer than the blade. The style is short and straight with no collar on the stigma. It is less common, but has a range similar to that of greenish-flowered wintergreen although it ranges farther west in Alas.

ARCTIC WINTERGREEN, LARGE-FLOWERED WINTERGREEN
Pyrola grandiflora Radius

A basal cluster of thick, glossy, rounded leaves that are dark green above, paler below, and usually whitened along the veins, gives rise to a short scape, 5–24 cm (2–10 in.) tall, with one or two small bracts. Relatively large flowers, more than 2 cm (3/4 in.) across, have sepals longer than broad, and white or pinkish petals with dark veins. Anthers are yellow and the styles long, somewhat curved at maturity, with a ring below the five stigma lobes. This is a rather common plant of open boreal woodland, and sheltered, sunny tundra slopes. It ranges throughout most of our area, farther north than other pyrolas.

ONE-SIDED PYROLA, ONE-SIDED WINTERGREEN
Orthilia secunda (L.) House
Syn. *Pyrola secunda* L.

This common plant is easily recognizable, being different from other members of the genus in that the small white to greenish flowers are borne along one side of the 7.5–15 cm (3–6 in.) scapes. Also, the leaves are distributed, not basally, but along the lower part of the stem. They are usually yellowish-green, and of very variable shape and serration of the edges. The style lacks a collar below the stigma, which is five-lobed.

Circumpolar, this species is quite frequent in moist thickets and woodland throughout our area and Alas.

ERICACEAE Heath Family

BOG ROSEMARY, WILD ROSEMARY
Andromeda polifolia L.

Occasionally branched, erect stems may be 10–75 cm (4–30 in.) high, with alternate, leathery leaves that are narrowly elliptic to linear in shape, and rolled under at the edges. The lower surface is noticeably whitish. Globe-shaped pink flowers hang from long pedicels, in a small umbel at the end of each branch. The corolla is up to 1 cm (3/8 in.) long, urn-shaped, with five short, recurved lobes at the mouth. This is an attractive evergreen plant of sphagnum bogs and acid swamps. It is circumboreal, and is locally abundant in suitable habitats throughout our area, blooming from late May until August. *Andromeda*, like many others of the Heath Family, contains the toxic compound andromedotoxin, which lowers blood pressure and causes breathing difficulty.

ALPINE BEARBERRY
Arctostaphylos alpina (L.) Spreng.

This is a prostrate shrub, usually less than 15 cm (6 in.) tall, with very noticeably shredded, papery, reddish bark. The firm leaves turn bright red in the fall, and are oval, about 4 cm (1 1/2 in.) long, with the greatest width near the tip. The edges are round-toothed, the veins conspicuous. Very narrow, urn-shaped flowers are pinkish, and less than 6 mm (1/4 in.) long. The fruit is a purplish-black, drupe-like berry containing five stony nutlets. It is juicy, but rather insipid in flavour, and is improved by cooking. This is a circumpolar species known in our area from the Arctic coastal region through Alas. except the lowlands of the Yukon River, and from c. and south-central Yukon. It is a plant of the barren peaty soil of tundra or alpine habitats, where it may be found in flower almost as soon as the snow has left.

RED BEARBERRY
Arctostaphylos rubra (Rehd. & Wils.) Fern.
A species very similar to *A. alpina* (which
see), it is often included as a subspecies, but
its leaves are deciduous, larger and thinner,
turning bright red in the fall. The berries are
larger and bright red when ripe. It occurs
quite commonly in moist open forests and
rocky tundra in our area.

BEARBERRY, KINNIKINNICK
Arctostaphylos uva-ursi (L.) Spreng.
The bark on the long, trailing stems is dark brown, and somewhat shredded. The flowers, in small terminal racemes, have urn-shaped corollas that are white to pink and the brilliant red berries may be nearly 12 mm (1/2 in.) in diameter. The berries are edible, though dry and mealy. Usually the small leathery leaves are less than 2.5 cm (1 in.) long, generally obovate, and blunt to rounded at their tips. This evergreen mat-like shrub is abundant on rocky outcrops, as well as the dry floor of open woods, throughout our area.

WESTERN MOSS HEATHER, WHITE MOSS HEATHER
Cassiope mertensiana (Bong.) D. Don
The tough, branched stems, up to 30 cm (12 in.) tall, are covered by many opposite, distinctly four-ranked leaves lying close to the stem, that are ovate-lanceolate, up to 5 mm (3/16 in.) long and grooved only at the extreme base. One to a few bell-shaped flowers, up to 1 cm (3/8 in.) long, are borne near the branch tip. Reddish sepals up to 3 mm (1/8 in.) long are ovate and entire. The tubular corolla has lobes much shorter than the tube. This is a locally common,

matted, evergreen shrub that covers rocks on the mountain slopes from timberline upward. It occurs in extreme n.w. BC, near Atlin, in the Cassiar Mtns. near the Yukon–BC border, and in the n. BC Rockies.

ALASKA MOSS HEATHER

Harrimanella stelleriana (Pall.) Colville
Syn. *Cassiope stelleriana* (Pall.) DC.
This diffuse, matted, evergreen shrub
has low, spreading branches, up to 15
cm (6 in.) tall. The very numerous
leaves are alternate and linear-lanceolate
and, unlike those of the other species of
Cassiope in our area, are spreading (not
appressed). The solitary, campanulate
flowers, about 5 mm (3/16 in.) long, are
borne on short pedicels. Sepals, about 3
mm (1/8 in.) long, are reddish. The
petals are white or pink-tinged, lobed
about halfway to the base. This is essen-

tially a plant of rocky slopes and alpine meadows and bogs at or above timberline. It occurs in extreme n.w. BC and s.w. Yukon, and in the Cassiar Mtns. near
the Yukon–BC border. Another species, CLUBMOSS MOUNTAIN HEATHER,
C. lycopodioides (Pall.) D. Don, is distinguished by its extremely slender stem
with tightly appressed leaves. It occurs in the Coast Mtns. adjacent to the Alaska
Panhandle.

WHITE MOUNTAIN HEATHER, ARCTIC WHITE HEATHER

Cassiope tetragona (L.) D. Don
A low, evergreen, alpine shrub
with ascending branches up to
30 cm (12 in.) tall, it is com-
pletely covered with numerous
6 mm (1/4 in.)-long leaves.
These are opposite, four-ranked
and very thick, with a deep fur-
row on the back. It is this fur-
row that unmistakably distin-
guishes this species from *C.
mertensiana* (which see), which
it otherwise resembles. The
campanulate flowers, one to a few near the branch tips, have pedicels up to
2.5 cm (1 in.) long. The ovate, about 3 mm (1/8 in.) long sepals are reddish.
The white or pinkish, 1 cm (3/8 in.) corolla has lobes less than halfway to the
base. On rocky slopes, alpine meadows and tundra above timberline to at least
1,800 m (6,000 ft.), this attractive shrub is circumpolar and is found abundantly
throughout the whole of our area.

LEATHER-LEAF, CASSANDRA

Chamaedaphne calyculata (L.)
Moench

This is a low, evergreen, branching
shrub up to 60 cm (24 in.) tall
with brown scaly stems. Oblong to
lanceolate, alternate, leathery
leaves up to 5 cm (2 in.) long, have
densely scaled lower surfaces.
Flowers, in the axils of the upper
leaves, form a one-sided, terminal,
leafy inflorescence. The calyx, subtended by two small bractlets, is
about one-third the length of the
corolla, which is up to 6 mm (1/4 in.) long, white, cylindrical and slightly narrowed at the throat. This shrub of sphagnum bogs and muskeg, often forming
dense thickets, is circumpolar in range; it occurs through c. Alas., in n. and c.
Yukon, the Mackenzie basin and e., and in a few locations in n. BC.

NORTHERN LABRADOR TEA

Ledum palustre L.
Syn. *L. decumbens* (Ait.) Lodd.

This evergreen shrub grows to a height of 10–50 cm
(4–20 in.). The elliptical leaves are alternate, often
appearing bunched or whorled. They are thick and leathery and dotted with resinous glands, glossy dark green
above, with rusty-woolly lower surfaces. Numerous white
flowers, in showy clusters, are about 1 cm (3/8 in.) wide
with five petals, and usually 10 stamens. The pedicels
have reddish hairs. This is a frequenter of swamps and
bogs, but it may also be found in drier, rocky places in
the mountains to at least 1,650 m (5,400 ft.). It ranges
through Alas. and the Yukon, in a few locations in extreme n. BC, and e.
through the Mackenzie basin. Another species, LABRADOR TEA, *L. groen-
landicum* Oeder, differs in
that it is taller (up to 1.2 m/
4 ft.), has longer leaves (up to
6 cm/2 1/2 in.), and fewer
stamens, and the pedicels
have white hairs. Ranging
from e. Alas., this species is
found throughout our area
and s. through BC.

BOG LAUREL, SWAMP LAUREL
Kalmia polifolia Wang.

Branched stems form loose mats 30–60 cm (12–24 in.) high. Leaves, dense in the upper part, are opposite, lanceolate, shiny above and pale beneath, with rolled-in margins. Branches are topped with umbels of crimson to rose-pink, saucer-shaped flowers on long, arching pedicels. The corolla is five-lobed, and about 1.5 cm (5/8 in.) in diameter. Ten arched anther-filaments are bent outwards, and the anthers are tucked into the corolla. The slightest touch will make the filaments whip the anther upward and inward to dust the visiting insect with pollen. The genus is named for Peter Kalm, a pupil of Linnaeus, who travelled in N. Amer. from 1748 to 1751. This plant is found in acid bogs throughout c. and s. Yukon, the upper Mackenzie basin e., and s. through BC.

ALPINE AZALEA
Loiseleuria procumbens (L.) Desv.

A much-branched, matted dwarf shrub, it has minute, opposite, leathery leaves that are elliptical in shape. Few campanulate flowers in terminal clusters are short-pedicelled with a pink corolla, having spreading, pointed lobes up to 5 mm (3/16 in.) long. It may be locally quite common in alpine and arctic tundra, gravelly slopes and peaty soils, in the mountains to at least 1,800 m (6,000 ft.). Circumpolar, it ranges through most of Alas., and throughout our area, except for n.e. BC and the n. Dist. of Mackenzie.

BOG CRANBERRY

Oxycoccus microcarpus Turcz.
Syn. *Vaccinium oxycoccos* L.

This is a tiny, creeping plant with thin stems that are usually found threading their way over, or through, sphagnum moss. Alternate, elliptic to ovate leaves, not more than 1 cm (3/8 in.) long, have strongly revolute margins. They are shiny deep green above, grey-white below. Small pinkish flowers, on very slender, arched pedicels, are deeply four-lobed, the lobes strongly recurved. These are followed by round, pale pink to purple berries often 1 cm or more in diameter. They are edible and make good jam, and are certainly not bitter, though the interpretation of the Greek "oxycoccus" is "bitter-berried." Circumboreal in range, it inhabits peat bogs through most of Alas., the Yukon and n. BC, but is rare in the Mackenzie basin and e., and on the n. coast.

YELLOW MOUNTAIN HEATHER, YELLOW MOUNTAIN HEATH

Phyllodoce glanduliflora (Hook.) Cov.
This is a low, matted, dwarf evergreen shrub with rather erect branches, up to 35 cm (14 in.) tall. Linear, yellowish-green leaves, up to 12 mm (1/2 in.) long with revolute margins, are clustered tightly together toward the tips of the branches. Yellowish to greenish-white urn-shaped flowers, one to several, are borne in clusters at the branch tips, each on a pedicel about 3 cm (1 3/16 in.) long. Calyx, corolla and pedicels are all covered in minute glandular-pubescent hairs. The fruit is a globose capsule more or less enclosed by the persistent calyx. Found on rather dry mountain slopes and rocky ledges in the open, at or above timberline, it occurs in n.w. BC between the Alaska and Yukon borders, in the adjacent region in s.w. Yukon, and in the s.w. Mackenzie Mtns.

PINK MOUNTAIN HEATHER, PINK MOUNTAIN HEATH, RED MOUNTAIN HEATHER

Phyllodoce empetriformis (Sm.) D. Don.
A low, evergreen, much-branched, matted, dwarf shrub with erect branches, it is very similar in form to *P. glanduliflora* (which see). The leaves of this species are much the same shape as the other, but a darker green. The flowers are a deep rose-pink colour, not constricted at the mouth, but bell-shaped, and not pubescent. The fruit exceeds the calyx in length. This species ranges in the mountains n. and e. of the Yukon River, and s. of 65° N.L., in the s.w. in the Haines and White Pass regions of BC and the Yukon, in the Mackenzie Mtns. adjacent to the Yukon border and s. along the Rockies.

LAPLAND ROSEBAY

Rhododendron lapponicum (L.) Wahlenb.

A much-branched dwarf shrub, it is usually erect, often only 5 cm (2 in.) high, seldom more than 30 cm (12 in.), but sometimes up to 60 cm (24 in.) in sheltered places. Close-ranked, oblong-elliptic leaves, 1–2 cm (3/8–3/4 in.) long, are dark green with rust-coloured scales, especially beneath. From one to five bright purple, fragrant flowers, 1–5 cm (3/8–2 in.) wide, appear in terminal clusters at the ends of short thick branchlets. Found on dry, rocky tundra and limestone slopes (a surprising fact in such an acid-loving genus), it is circumpolar, extending from n. and w. Alas., throughout the Yukon and extreme n. BC, and e. across n. Canada.

DWARF BLUEBERRY, DWARF BILBERRY
Vaccinium caespitosum Michx.

This is a tiny, densely branched, dwarf shrub, up to 30 cm (12 in.) tall, that spreads widely by creeping rootstocks. Young twigs are slightly angled and often yellowish-green, sometimes reddish. Obovate leaves, nearly sessile, usually less than 2.5 cm (1 in.) long, are notched toward the tip, shiny on both sides and uniformly serrate. The flowers, with tubular, five-lobed, pink or white corollas, up to 6 mm (1/4 in.) long, occur singly in the leaf axils on short pedicels. The fruit is a berry, up to 8 mm (5/16 in.) broad, light blue to blackish-blue with a pale bloom. It is sweet and edible. In open forests, on wet mountain meadows and slopes, and on moist rocky outcrops and alpine tundra, dwarf blueberry may be found, often locally abundant. It ranges through the mountains of the Kenai Peninsula and the Alaska Range and from central s. and s.w. Yukon, s. through BC.

ALPINE BLUEBERRY, BOG HUCKLEBERRY, WHORTLEBERRY, BILBERRY
Vaccinium uliginosum L.

A rather low, deciduous shrub, up to 50 cm (20 in.) tall, it is much branched, with the branches greyish-red and young twigs yellowish-green. Leaves, usually obovate, up to 3 cm (1 1/4 in.) long, are firm and have entire margins. They are green above, paler beneath and strongly veined. Flowers are in clusters of up to four in the leaf axils, with pink, ovoid to urn-shaped corollas. The fruit is a globular berry, up to 8 mm (5/16 in.) in diameter, blue black with a bloom, sweet and edible. This is a shrub of sphagnum bogs and wet muskeg areas. Circumboreal in range, it is found throughout our area, often locally common. Another species, MOUNTAIN BILBERRY, BLACK HUCKLEBERRY, or TALL BLUE-BERRY, *V. membranaceum* Dougl., is found in the Cassiar Mtns. and the

Rockies ranging s. It is a densely branched shrub up to 2 m (6 ft.) tall. The young branches are smooth, yellow green and somewhat angled. Ovate, pointed leaves have serrate margins and are up to 6 mm (1/4 in.) long. Single flowers in the leaf axils have creamy pink corollas. The fruit, 1 cm (3/8 in.) in diameter, is globose and purplish-black without a bloom, and tastes good. This is a species of dry mountain slopes and open forests.

ROCK CRANBERRY, MOUNTAIN CRANBERRY, LINGONBERRY

Vaccinium vitis-idaea L.
The leathery leaves, almost sessile, up to 15 mm (9/16 in.) long, are obovate, dark glossy green above and paler beneath, with margins slightly revolute. They are distinctly dotted with black bristly points beneath. Bell-shaped white or rose-pink flowers, with the corolla four-cleft to the middle, are about 5 mm (3/16 in.) long.

A bright red berry, up to 1 cm (3/8 in.) in diameter, is edible, but rather acid, and more palatable when cooked. This low, evergreen, mat-forming, dwarf shrub, up to 20 cm (8 in.) tall, somewhat resembles *Arctostaphylos uva-ursi* (which see). Both may be found in open woods, but rock cranberry is also found in drier, open, rocky areas. Circumboreal in range, it is common in many parts of Alas. and throughout much of our area.

DIAPENSIACEAE
Diapensia Family

LAPLAND DIAPENSIA
Diapensia lapponica L.
Syn. *D. obovata* (Fr. Schm.) Nakai
A variable, small, tufted, alpine plant, often forming dense cushions, it has tiny, thick, obovate to oblanceolate leaves that are shiny green, with a very distinct mid-vein. The flowers, large compared to the leaves, have small yellowish sepals, and a white five-lobed corolla. They face upwards, borne on reddish pedicels well above the leaves. This is a plant of rocky, alpine situations, up to at least 1,500 m (5,000 ft.). It occurs in the mountains of most of Alas., extending e. to the Richardson Mtns. in the extreme north, and in the mountains of the w. and c. regions of the Yukon.

PRIMULACEAE Primrose Family

ROCK JASMINE, SWEET-FLOWERED ANDROSACE
Androsace chamaejasme Wulf.
This attractive member of the Primrose Family has rosettes of leaves on perennial, prostrate stems, forming mats up to 15 cm (6 in.) across. Each rosette gives rise to a single, leafless scape up to 10 cm (4 in.) high, which bears an umbel of small, white, yellow-eyed, fragrant flowers. Rock jasmine is found on rocky slopes, on tundra and up to 1,550 m (5,100 ft.) in the mountains. It ranges through the mountains of Alas. and e. along the Arctic coast of the Yukon and the Dist. of Mackenzie, in the s.w. Yukon and in the upper Mackenzie basin.

PIGMY FLOWER, FAIRY CANDELABRA
Androsace septentrionalis L.

This annual member of the Primrose Family has thin flowering stems of unequal length up to 30 cm (12 in.) high, each topped by an open umbel of many small white flowers, rising from a rosette of small, entire or toothed, linear-lanceolate, reddish-green leaves. Found in dry, rocky, or sandy places, up to 1,800 m (6,000 ft.) in the mountains, it is circumpolar, common in s. Yukon and n. BC, and ranging through most of our area.

NORTHERN SHOOTING STAR
Dodecatheon frigidum Cham. & Schlecht.

From a cluster of petioled, smooth leaves with wavy margins, up to 15 cm (6 in.) long, rises a leafless scape that may be as much as 30 cm (12 in.) high. One to several nodding flowers, borne in terminal umbels, have pointed, reflexed corolla lobes that are magenta to lavender in colour. The capsules, about 8 mm (5/16 in.) long, are held erect. In meadows, moist tundra, heathlands and open forest, it ranges over most of the Yukon and Alas. (except Alas. Penin. and the Aleutians), extreme n. BC and in the mountains of the Dist. of Mackenzie. Another species, FEW-FLOWERED SHOOTING STAR, *D. pulchellum* (Raf.) Merr., which is extremely variable, differs from the above in that the stamen filaments are united into a yellow tube. It is usually found along the Alaskan coast and in e. Alas., as well as the adjoining west-central Yukon, and in the upper Mackenzie basin in wet meadows and saline flats.

ARCTIC DOUGLASIA
Douglasia arctica Hook.
This is a smaller plant than *D. gormanii* (which see). Growing on rocky, mossy slopes in loose tufts, it differs from *D. gormanii* mainly in its leaves, which are smooth above and ciliated below but not covered in stellate hairs as in the latter species. It is found only in a small region in e. Alas., in n. Yukon and in the Richardson Mtns. of the n.w. Dist. of Mackenzie.

DOUGLASIA
Douglasia gormanii Constance
Closely packed rosettes of overlapping oblanceolate leaves up to 1 cm (3/8 in.) long form dense cushions up to about 5 cm (2 in.) high. The leaves are pubescent on the lower surface and the margins, with stellate hairs. Each rosette bears a single, comparatively large flower, with a deeply five-lobed corolla of rose pink. Often the whole cushion of leaves may be obscured by a beautiful dome of pink blooms, mid-May to late June. This small and extremely attractive alpine plant may be found on stony slopes in the high mountains of c. Alas., c. and s.w. Yukon and n.w. BC, up to at least 1,800 m (6,000 ft.). It grows only in this region.

SEA MILK-WORT
Glaux maritima L.

The upright stems, about 30 cm (12 in.) tall, are crowded with opposite, fleshy, stalkless leaves. Tiny white or pinkish flowers, borne in the leaf-axils, appear May–July. This is primarily a plant of saline habitats, commonly along sea shores. It may also be found around alkaline ponds in the vicinity of Whitehorse, in the Salt Plain w. of Fort Smith, along the s. shore of Great Slave Lake and on the upper Mackenzie River.

NORTHERN PRIMROSE
Primula borealis Duby

The leaves in basal rosettes may be up to 6 cm (2 3/8 in.) long with petioles usually longer than the blades, which have shallowly toothed or entire margins. Scapes up to 15 cm (6 in.) tall bear umbels of two to seven flowers. The lilac (rarely white) corolla, about 1.5 cm (5/8 in.) across, has a yellow centre and tube, and obcordate lobes. This highly variable plant may be found in moist, often saline, meadows or sea shores on either side of the Bering Strait, along the n. coast of Alas. and the Yukon, extending to e. of the Mackenzie delta.

WEDGE-LEAVED PRIMROSE, PIXIE EYES
Primula cuneifolia Ledeb.

From a basal rosette of smooth, cuneiform leaves, dentate at the apex, rises a scape, up to 5 cm (2 in.) tall, bearing a single flower, or two or more, in an umbel. The five lobes of the pink to rose or violet corolla are deeply divided. This delicate and attractive plant is only found in our area in wet meadows in the mountains of n.w. BC, and coastal areas throughout Alas., except the n. coast.

GREENLAND PRIMROSE
Primula egaliksensis Wormsk.
This has small, obovate leaves with entire margins, up to 2 cm (3/4 in.) long, and a thin scape that may be as much as 15 cm (6 in.) tall. The white to lilac corolla, about 6 mm (1/4 in.) across, has deeply cleft lobes, shorter than the tube; it is yellow in the centre and in the tube. Found in wet meadows and on stream banks and lake shores in calcareous areas, it appears in s. Yukon, n.w. BC, in the extreme n. of the Yukon, in the Mackenzie basin, around Great Bear and Great Slave lakes, and in the mountains of n. and w. Alas. extending into the Aleutians.

ARCTIC PRIMROSE
Primula eximia Greene
A basal rosette of thin, narrowly lanceolate leaves, 5–7 cm (2–2 3/4 in.) long, entire or irregularly dentate, with broad petioles, gives rise to a stout scape, up to 20 cm (8 in.) tall, that bears an umbel of three to five flowers. The corolla is purple with a white eye, the tube much longer than the calyx. This highly variable species may be found in wet meadows and on stream banks in w. Alas. It also occurs in the Richardson Mtns. near the Yukon Territory–Dist. of Mackenzie border.

NORTHERN STARFLOWER
Trientalis arctica Fisch.
Syn. *T. europaea* L.
This is a variable species, but the form that is common in our area has obovate leaves, rounded at the apex (not lanceolate, as in the rarer form). They are up to 5 cm (2 in.) long, and arranged in a terminal cluster with smaller leaves on the stem below. The flowers, on slender pedicels, are white with six or more pointed corolla lobes. It grows in clusters from creeping rootstocks in moist open forests, thickets, meadows or tundra in c. and s.w. Yukon, in n.w. BC, around the west end of Great Slave Lake, and throughout s. and c. Alas.

PLUMBAGINACEAE Leadwort Family

THRIFT
Armeria maritima (Mill.) Willd.
This plant forms dense tussocks on cliffs on lake and sea shores and gravelly tundra. The leaves are linear, greyish green and rather fleshy. Scapes, often several on a tussock, may be up to 30 cm (12 in.) tall, terminating in a small round head of pink flowers. This is a variable species that is circumpolar. It extends along the n. coast of Alas., the Yukon and the Dist. of Mackenzie, with locations around Great Slave Lake and in the Mackenzie River valley.

GENTIANACEAE Gentian Family

FELWORT, NORTHERN GENTIAN
Gentiana acuta Michx.
Syn. *Gentianella amarella* ssp. *acuta* (L.)
Boerner

The erect stems may grow to as much as 60 cm (24 in.) tall. They may be single, or have ascending branches; the sessile, lanceolate leaves are in opposite pairs, basal and up the stem. Flowers are often numerous, in small, stalked clusters, in the axils of the upper leaves. The calyx is cleft nearly to the base with narrow, acute lobes. The acute corolla lobes are mauve to purple or lilac, rarely white. This is quite a common gentian of moist stream banks, meadows and open forest.
Circumboreal, it occurs in many regions of c. and s. Yukon and n. BC, in the Mackenzie River drainage system n. to the Arctic Circle, in the Great Slave Lake region, and s. Alas.

WHITISH GENTIAN
Gentiana algida Pall.

This interesting gentian has smooth yellowish-green stems 15–20 cm (6–8 in.) tall, with linear-oblong sheathing leaves that have a single vein. Flowers, one to three in terminal cymes, have a calyx with five unequal lobes, and a funnel-form, up-to-5 cm (2 in.) corolla that is white to cream, and mottled or striped with purple. Found in meadows and on stony slopes in the mountains at least up to 1,400 m (4,500 ft.), it ranges through c. and coastal areas of w. Alas. and the Aleutians, into west-central and s.w. Yukon, and is common in some locations in the Ogilvie Mtns. and near Kluane Lake.

WINDMILL FRINGED-GENTIAN
Gentianopsis dentosa (Rottb.) Ma

Erect stems, rising from a basal rosette of oblanceolate leaves, are up to 60 cm (24 in.) tall, and may be branched from the axils of the lanceolate stem leaves. A long pedicel, extending from the top pair of stem leaves, bears a single terminal flower. The tubular corolla is up to 5 cm (2 in.) long and deep blue. Found in open forests, meadows and tundra, it ranges from c. Alas. into s.w. Yukon.

GLAUCOUS GENTIAN
Gentiana glauca Pall.

The stem, up to 15 cm (6 in.) tall, rises from a basal rosette of smooth, obovate, yellowish-green leaves, and has one to three pairs of connate stem leaves below the bracts of the inflorescence. Calyx lobes are unequal and acute. The corolla, about 1.5 cm (5/8 in.) long, is blue, dark blue, greenish-blue, or yellowish, with ovate lobes much shorter than the tube. This is found in alpine and subalpine meadows throughout Alas., the Yukon and n. BC, extending e. to the east slope of the Mackenzie and Richardson Mtns.

FOUR-PETALLED GENTIAN
Gentianella propinqua (Richards.) Gillet
Syn. *Gentiana propinqua* Richards.
This is an annual with smooth stems up to 40 cm (16 in.) long, either erect or ascending, usually branched. The basal rosette leaves are spatulate, stem leaves lanceolate to oblong, up to 3.5 cm (1 3/8 in.) long, and not connate. There are often many flowers, in cymes. The calyx, up to 12 mm (1/2 in.) long, has lobes longer than the tube. The corolla, up to 2 cm (3/4 in.) long with four lobes that are blue fading to white, has a greenish-blue tube. Found in open forests, dry mountain slopes and on tundra to at least 1,800 m (6,000 ft.) throughout Alas. and the Yukon, it ranges e. to the Mackenzie River and to the Coppermine River in the n., and s. along the Rockies in BC.

MOSS GENTIAN
Gentiana prostrata Haenke
This is a smooth, light green plant, with an erect stem, simple or branched from the base. It has three to four pairs of ovate leaves on each stem. The single, terminal flowers have a blue corolla no more than 1.5–2 cm (3/4 in.) long, with four or five lance-ovate lobes. These only open in bright sunny weather. A species of bogs and meadows up to 1,800 m (6,000 ft.), it is found in the mountains of Alas. and the Yukon, e. through the Mackenzie Mtns., and s. in the Rockies.

STAR GENTIAN
Lomatogonium rotatum (L.) Fries

This attractive plant varies from an unbranched, single-flowered stem no more than 3 cm (1 1/4 in.) high, to one with many flowers on strongly ascending branches on a stem that may be 50 cm (20 in.) or more tall. The basal leaves soon wither; the opposite stem leaves are oblanceolate below, linear above. The sepals are acute, similar to the upper leaves. The wheel-shaped corolla, about the same length as the calyx, is purplish-blue, light blue or (rarely) white. It is found in wet meadows, on stream banks and sandy sea shores. It is quite common throughout most of Alas. except the s.w., on the n. coast of the Yukon and Dist. of Mackenzie, and it may be found in the Yukon River valley and in the s.w. part of the territory.

MENYANTHACEAE
Buckbean Family

BUCKBEAN

Menyanthes trifoliata L.

The smooth, fleshy leaves, each with three elliptical leaflets, have long petioles, the lower end of which is much widened to form a clasping stipule. The leaves are basally clustered at the foot of a 15–30 cm (6–12 in.) flower stem. Numerous fringed flowers are white, occasionally pink-flushed, and crowded in a short raceme. The calyx is deeply five- or six-parted, as is the corolla. The inner face of the flat corolla lobes is covered with white hair-like projections that are very conspicuous. Some of the flowers in a single raceme have five stamens longer than, and almost obscuring, the petal; in others the stamens are short, so that the style is evident. This is an easily recognized and sometimes common plant of bogs and swamps with stout, far-spreading rootstocks. It is circumpolar in range, and is widespread from Alas. throughout our area except in the extreme north.

APOCYNACEAE Dogbane Family

DOGBANE

Apocynum androsaemifolium L.

This is a tall plant (up to 60 cm/24 in.), with freely branched, slender stems that may be glabrous or hairy. When broken they exude an acrid white juice. The opposite-paired leaves are egg-shaped, with a short, pointed tip. Characteristically, the leaves droop during the heat of the day. The small pink bell-shaped flowers are attractively lined with deeper pink honey guides. Five

stamens are ranked around a pistil with unusual nectaries at its base. Long, slender and pendulous fruiting capsules may be up to 7 cm (2 3/4 in.) long or more. The seed has a tuft of pale brown silky hairs 2.5 cm (1 in.) long. Widespread throughout the north of the continent, but not in the far north, it extends into e. Alas., and throughout s. Yukon, n. BC and the upper Mackenzie River drainage system. Dogbane may be found in rather dry places, on roadsides and in open woodland.

POLEMONIACEAE Phlox Family

ALASKAN PHLOX

Phlox alaskensis Jordal

The much-branched stems are covered in the lower part with the remains of leaves and leaf bases. The linear-lanceolate leaves, with acuminate tips, are sticky with gland-tipped, pubescent hairs. Single (occasionally two) flowers at the tip of each branch have corolla tubes as long as the deeply lobed calyx. The lobes of the corolla, pale to dark pink fading to blue, are broad and rounded. The whole, wheel-shaped flower is about 2 cm (7/8 in.) in diameter. A matted, showy plant, it forms low cushions on rocky limestone hillsides in

the mountains, up to at least 1,800 m (6,000 ft.). It is found only in n. Alas. and the adjacent Yukon, as well as some locations in the Ogilvie and Richardson Mtns. w. of the Mackenzie delta.

TALL JACOB'S LADDER

Polemonium acutiflorum Willd.

Many erect, unbranched stems up to 40 cm (16 in.) or more tall rise from a tuft of long-petioled, pinnately compound leaves, each with up to 27 elliptic to lanceolate smooth leaflets. The showy, campanulate flowers, with pointed corolla lobes up to 2 cm (3/4 in.) long, vary in colour from pinkish, through lavender to bluish-violet. This rather variable species is quite common throughout Alas., the Yukon and n. BC, ranging e. to the Mackenzie and Richardson Mtns., in wet meadows and along stream banks.

NORTHERN JACOB'S LADDER
Polemonium boreale Adams
This is rather similar to *P. pulcherrimum* (which see), but is much shorter, having sticky-pubescent stems seldom taller than 15 cm (6 in.). Leaves, mostly basal, have 9–12 pairs of elliptic leaflets. The showy flowers, in a dense corymb, are 1.5–2 cm (3/4 in.) long and purplish-blue with a yellow tube. Found in calcareous, sandy or gravelly places, often near animal burrows, it ranges through n. Alas. e. along the Arctic coast to the Coppermine River, through c. Alas. and the adjacent Yukon, to at least 2,100 m (7,000 ft.) in the St. Elias Mtns., in the Richardson and Mackenzie Mtns., and n.w. BC.

SHOWY JACOB'S LADDER
Polemonium pulcherrimum Hook.
This is a tufted plant, 5–30 cm (2–12 in.) high, with viscid-pubescent basal leaves, each having 11–23 pointed-oval leaflets. Stems, more or less erect, are sparingly branched with a few reduced leaves. Flowers are borne in a rather open cluster on long slender pedicels. Corollas are short-tubed, with broad lobes about as long as, or up to twice as long as, the tube. They are lavender blue, contrasting with the vivid orange ring at the base of the cup. Pure white-flowered specimens of showy Jacob's ladder are not uncommon. Found in dry, rocky and sandy places, it ranges throughout e. and s. Alas. and the Yukon, s. through the interior of BC and e. to the Mackenzie delta, the w. shore of Great Bear Lake and the eastern slopes of the Mackenzie Mtns. Flowering early in June in most of these localities, by mid-July it is in seed.

HYDROPHYLLACEAE Waterleaf Family

SCORPION-WEED
Phacelia franklinii (R. Br.) Gray
Single, leafy, hairy and sometimes branched stems up to 70 cm (28 in.) high are topped by curled cymes. Hirsute leaves, mostly on the stem, deeply pinnately lobed and up to 5 cm (2 in.) long, are only slightly reduced upward. The corolla, purplish fading to cream, is rotate-campanulate. Scorpion-weed is found on dry, sandy, disturbed or burnt-over areas, often by roadsides in s. Yukon, the western slopes of the Mackenzie Mtns. and around Great Slave Lake.

HAIRY SCORPION-WEED
Phacelia mollis Macbr.
A soft-hairy, velvety plant, the solitary stem has coarsely toothed, lanceolate leaves. Rounded lobes of the corolla, about twice as long as the tube, are blue, lavender or pale yellow. Stamens are about twice the length of the corolla. This is quite distinctive from the other species of *Phacelia* in our area, *P. franklinii* (which see), the stamens of which do not project beyond (or only slightly beyond) the corolla. A species native only to east-central Alas. and the adjacent Yukon, where it is quite rare, extending up the Yukon River at least to the Pelly River, and in the White Pass region of n. BC, it is found on dry slopes and roadsides.

BORAGINACEAE Borage Family

ARCTIC FORGET-ME-NOT

Eritrichium aretioides (Cham. & Schlecht.) DC.
This is a small, densely tufted plant, the ovate
to oblanceolate, acute leaves of which are
densely covered in straight hairs. Flowering
stems up to 10 cm (4 in.) long, with four or
five stem leaves, are topped with a short, dense
raceme of tiny flowers, less than 1 cm (3/8 in.)
in diameter, the deep blue corolla lobes centred
with a yellowish or reddish tube. Occurring on
dry mountain slopes and on sandy tundra soil,
it ranges through n.e. and c. Alas. into west-
central and n. Yukon.

SHOWY ARCTIC FORGET-ME-NOT

Eritrichium splendens Kearney

Flowering stems, about 10 cm (4 in.) high, bear an open raceme of a few, bright blue flowers about 1 cm (3/8 in.) in diameter, with broadly obovate petals. This can be distinguished easily from the other species, *E. aretioides* (which see), by the fruit: the four nutlets each have a crown of jagged teeth, those of the other having nearly smooth teeth. This is a rare species of alpine slopes, growing only in Alas., the n. and s.w. Yukon and the Richardson Mtns.

STICKSEED

Lappula squarrosa (Retz.) Dumart.
Syn.*L. myosotis* Moench.
Syn. *L. echinata* Gilib.

Stems, 50 cm (20 in.) or more tall, are usually branched and have lanceolate, sessile leaves. The flowers are tiny; the corollas, with five rounded lobes, are no more than 3 mm (1/8 in.) in diameter. The fruit, a nutlet, has two rows of marginal prickles. This is a rather weedy plant, found mostly in disturbed areas and dry, sandy, waste places. The minute prickles on the nutlets attach themselves to the fur of animals and the clothes of humans, so that they are easily dispersed. The species is widespread from c. Alas. through s. Yukon and n. BC. Another, less robust, species, WESTERN STICKSEED, *L. occidentalis* (Wats.) Greene, or *L. redowskii* (Hornem.) Greene, is distinguished by having a single row of prickles on the nutlets. This is also widespread through our area.

TALL LUNGWORT, BLUEBELLS
Mertensiana paniculata (Ait.) G. Don

The curving stems may be up to 70 cm (28 in.). The leaves are rough-hairy, the lower ones long-petioled with a cordate-ovate to lanceolate-elliptic blade up to 15 cm (6 in.) long; the upper ones are sessile and shorter. The inflorescence is a dense cluster of pendant, deep blue to purplish-blue (rarely white) flowers. Corollas, 1.5 cm (5/8 in.) long, are funnel-shaped. This is an attractive plant of wet meadows and clearings, shady roadsides and stream banks, occasionally ascending to above timberline, and often growing in extensive clumps. It is very common throughout the Yukon and Alas. except the far north and in n. BC, extending to the Mackenzie River and Great Slave Lake. Another species, SEA LUNGWORT, *M. maritima* (L.) S.F. Gray, may be found on shingle sea beaches on the Arctic coast in our area. This has somewhat fleshy, glaucous, ovate or spatulate leaves and small purplish-pink, pale blue or, rarely, white flowers.

ALPINE FORGET-ME-NOT
Myosotis asiatica (Vestergr.) Schischk. & Serg.
Syn. *M. alpestris* Schm.

Single to several stems up to 25 cm (10 in.) tall rise from amongst a few, long-petioled, lanceolate, pubescent basal leaves. The stem leaves are alternate, shorter than the basal leaves and sessile. Tiny, bright blue to pale blue flowers with yellow centres are salver-shaped, 3–4 mm (1/8 in.) across, in dense clusters. This attractive plant is the state flower of Alaska. It occurs in moist alpine and subalpine meadows up to at least 1,600 m (5,300 ft.) throughout most of Alas. and our area, extending e. to the Mackenzie and Richardson Mtns.

LAMIACEAE Mint Family

WILD MINT, FIELD MINT
Mentha arvensis L.

An extremely variable species, it is easily recognized by its attractive fragrance. The stems may be simple or branched and up to 50 cm (20 in.) or more tall, rising from a creeping rootstock. The petioled leaves, ovate to lanceolate with serrate margins, are opposite up the stem. Flowers are borne in the axils of the leaves. Each has a light purple or pink corolla tube with three rounded lobes and a fourth that is wider and notched. The four long stamens and the pistil project beyond the mouth of the tube. Wild mint is a plant of wet places and river banks. It is widespread across N. Amer. and is found occasionally throughout our area s. of the Arctic Circle.

SKULLCAP
Scutellaria galericulata L.

Simple or branched stems, up to 40 cm (16 in.) tall, rise from creeping rhizomes. The opposite leaves are short-petioled, ovate or lanceolate, serrate and pubescent beneath. The flowers are borne singly in the axils of the middle and upper leaves. The corolla, blue to blue-violet and up to 2 cm (3/4 in.) long, has two lips, the upper lip having a broad hollow pouch (*galericulata* means "covered by a cup-like lid"). Widespread across the northern part of N. Amer., skullcap occurs in a number of locations in c. Alas., c. and s.e. Yukon, the upper Mackenzie basin and around Great Bear and Great Slave lakes. It is a plant of low marshy places, lake shores and stream banks.

SCROPHULARIACEAE
Figwort Family

PALE PAINTBRUSH, PALE INDIAN PAINTBRUSH

Castilleja caudata (Pennell) Rebr.
Syn. *C. pallida* (L) Spreng.

This species has a few to several erect or ascending stems up to 40 cm (16 in.) long, pubescent toward the upper half, and often branched. Leaves, the lower narrowly lanceolate, the upper with a distinct, long, tail-like tip, are finely pubescent below. The inflorescence has 5–12 flowers, each with hairy, greenish-yellow bracts that are usually entire. It occurs on stream banks, lake shores and tundra in most of Alas., and from s.w. to n. Yukon, extending e. in the Dist. of Mackenzie to Coronation Gulf and Great Bear Lake and s. to Great Slave Lake.

ELEGANT PAINTBRUSH, ELEGANT INDIAN PAINTBRUSH

Castilleja elegans Malte

Several ascending stems, branching from the base, up to 25 cm (10 in.) long, are pubescent, especially above. Pubescent leaves are linear and caudate; they are entire or frequently have a pair of lateral and linear lobes near the tip of the stem. The purplish bracts sometimes have yellowish tops. It is found in moist, calcareous tundra or on rocky or sandy lake shores n. of 67° N.L. in the Yukon, n. and c. Alas. and through the Dist. of Mackenzie.

NORTHERN PAINTBRUSH, NORTHERN INDIAN PAINTBRUSH

Castilleja hyperborea Pennell

Two or more, often many, stems rise from a much-branched woody base up to 15 cm (6 in.) in height. The inflorescence elongates to about one-third the length of the stem. Lower leaves are sometimes entire and lanceolate, the upper with one or two pairs of slender divergent lobes. The bracts are yellow or yellowish-white, and are more cleft than the leaves. Found on stony slopes in the mountains of n. and c. Alas. and the adjacent Yukon, it extends to the Mackenzie and Richardson Mtns. and along the Arctic coast to 125° W.L.

ROSY PAINTBRUSH, ROSY INDIAN PAINTBRUSH, MOUNTAIN PAINTBRUSH, MOUNTAIN INDIAN PAINTBRUSH

Castilleja parviflora Bong.

Many slim, 8–23 cm (3–9 in.)-tall, unbranched stems arise in a cluster from a semi-woody root crown. The flowers are enclosed by rose-pink bracts that are

deeply cleft into three to seven rather pointed, spreading lobes. The hairs on stem, leaves, and especially the inflorescence are never stiff and bristly, but always soft-woolly and either sparse or thick. This mountain species ranges from the s. coast of Alas. and the Panhandle s. in the Coast Mtns. It appears in our area in mountain meadows in the White Pass and the Haines Pass regions.

RAUP'S PAINTBRUSH, RAUP'S INDIAN PAINTBRUSH
Castilleja raupii Pennell

One to several slender, simple or branched, greenish to purplish stems, up to 40 cm (16 in.) tall, bear entire, linear-lanceolate leaves. These are 4–5 cm (1 1/2–2 in.) long, rarely lobed; finely pubescent on both sides, they also have cobwebby hairs. Bracts, ovate to lanceolate, are purple. The purple lower lip of the 2 cm (3/4 in.) corolla is about half as long as the upper one, which is green. On river banks and lake shores, this species is found from the Mt. McKinley region of Alas., and east-central Yukon, to the Mackenzie River valley, n. to its delta, e. from Great Slave Lake and s. to n. BC. A similar-shaped species, having yellowish bracts, is YUKON INDIAN PAINTBRUSH, *C. yukonis* Pennell. Not more than 25 cm (10 in.) tall, it has a yellowish-green corolla about 2 cm (3/4 in.) long, the upper lip very narrow and much larger than the three-lobed lower lip. On stony river banks and hillsides it may be found in the upper Yukon valley, the lower Pelly River and Kluane Lake regions of c. and s.w. Yukon.

COASTAL PAINTBRUSH, COASTAL INDIAN PAINTBRUSH
Castilleja unalaschensis (Cham. & Schlecht.) Malte

From a short, stout, scaly, many-headed caudex rise several stems, smooth below, soft-hairy above. Leaves are ovate to lanceolate, acute, pubescent on both sides and three- to five-veined. The yellow bracts are ovate; the lowest are entire, the upper occasionally have one or two pairs of lobes. It should be noted that the showy appearance of the paintbrushes is due to the colourful bracts, in the axils of which are the usually quite inconspicuous flowers. Very common in grassy meadows in s. and s.w. Yukon, it also occurs in the Haines and White Pass, Bennett Lake and Atlin areas in n.w. BC.

EYEBRIGHT

Euphrasia subarctica Raup
The simple or branched stems, up to 20 cm (8 in.) tall, have opposite, prominently toothed, ovate to obovate, pubescent leaves, lacking petioles. In the axils of the leaves are the tiny flowers. An irregular, lilac to whitish-purple corolla only just exceeds the calyx in length. This is a tiny plant of s.e. Alas., s.w. Yukon, n. Rockies in BC and s.w. Dist. of Mackenzie. It is found in bogs, on stream banks and in other wet places.

LAGOTIS, LITTLE WEASEL SNOUT

Lagotis glauca Gaertn.
Syn. *L. stelleri* (Cham. & Schlecht.) Rupr.
This has one to several stems, up to 20 cm (8 in.), rising from an ascending rhizome. The basal leaves are petiolate with oblanceolate blades that are crenate to dentate. Much smaller stem leaves are sessile and entire. A spike-like inflorescence bears many pale blue flowers, each supported by a small leafy bract. Occurring on moist, rocky alpine slopes and tundra, it ranges through Alas. and throughout the Yukon, reaching its eastern limit on the east slope of the Mackenzie and Richardson Mtns.

COMMON MONKEY FLOWER, YELLOW MONKEY FLOWER

Mimulus guttatus DC.

This highly variable species has erect stems that may be quite short or more than 50 cm (20 in.) tall. Opposite leaves, ovate with irregular dentate margins, are either smooth or soft-haired, the lower ones short-petioled, the upper ones sessile and somewhat clasping. The inflorescence is an open raceme of a few large showy flowers. The corolla, 3–4 cm (1 3/16–1 9/16 in.) long, is bright yellow, sometimes

crimson-spotted in the throat. The calyx lobes are uneven, the upper one being much larger than the others. Common monkey flower occurs in wet seepage areas, by streams and warm springs, mostly in the Coast Mtns. From c. and s. Alas., it ranges s. along the whole Pacific coast. It is found s. from the BC–Yukon border, in the s.w. Dist. of Mackenzie, s.e. along the Rockies, and s.e. Yukon to about Whitehorse.

CAPITATE LOUSEWORT, HEAD-SHAPED LOUSEWORT, FEW-FLOWERED LOUSEWORT

Pedicularis capitata Adams

A dwarf species with unbranched stems, it is seldom more than 15 cm (6 in.)

high and terminates in a head with two to four (rarely six) large flowers. Basal leaves are long-petioled, oblong in outline and pinnately compound, the leaflets again pinnately cleft. The one or two stem leaves are less dissected and shorter-petioled. Bracts are pinnately lobed and leaf-like, and the calyx lobes are also lobed. The corolla is creamy yellow, the upper lip sometimes becoming rose-coloured with age. The upper lip is large and curved with a short beak, the lower three-cleft. Found on rocky slopes, gravelly calcareous tundra and heath lands, it ranges throughout most of our area.

ELEPHANT-HEAD
Pedicularis groenlandica Retz.

An impressive spike bears red to purple-pink flowers that are unmistakable, bearing a distinct resemblance to an elephant's head and trunk. These top a sturdy, glabrous, reddish-purple stem 30–60 cm (12–24 in.) tall. The leaves (basal ones petioled, upper ones sessile) are deeply pinnatifid. This species of wet calcareous meadows has only appeared n. of 60° N.L. in one locality, near Watson Lake.

LABRADOR LOUSEWORT
Pedicularis labradorica Wirsing

A single stem, up to about 30 cm (12 in.) high, rises from a taproot, usually much branched from the base upwards. The lower leaves are pinnately cleft, gradually reduced upward. Five- to ten-flowered inflorescences are at first short, then elongated. The calyx is two-cleft. The corolla has a straight, yellow to reddish tube; the upper lip has two teeth near the tip, the lower lip is three-lobed. A common plant from Alas. e. across northern Canada, it does not extend very far s. into BC. It may be found in open mossy places, on tundra and up to 1,800 m (6,000 ft.) in the mountains.

WOOLLY LOUSEWORT
Pedicularis lanata Cham. & Schlecht.
Syn. *P. kanei* Durand
It has a simple, usually single, about 15 cm (6 in.)-tall stem rising from a thick yellow taproot. Numerous long-petioled, linear-lanceolate basal leaves are pinnately lobed. The inflorescence is densely white-woolly, the lower bracts longer than the flowers. The calyx has triangular acute teeth; the rose-coloured corolla has a straight galea and tube, teeth are lacking, and the lower lip is about as long as the upper and three-lobed. It is found in moist, stony tundra through most of our area, excluding n.w. BC. The roots are edible raw or boiled, according to Hultén.

LANGSDORF'S LOUSEWORT
Pedicularis langsdorfii Fisch.
Syn. *P. arctica* R. Br.
Stems may be solitary or numerous, arising from a stout rootstock. They are up to 30 cm (12 in.) tall, and woolly-villous above. Both basal and stem leaves are long-petioled and pinnately lobed into numerous crenate segments. The inflorescence is elongated, often longer than the vegetative portion of the stem. Lower bracts surpass the flowers; the upper ones are reduced. The galea of the prominently arched purple corolla about equals the tube in length and is beakless, bearing a

pair of slender teeth near the tip, unlike *P. lanata* (which see). The lower lip, three-lobed, is shorter than the upper. Found in alpine meadows and tundra, it extends e. along the Arctic coast from n.w. Alas. It ranges s. through the mountains of e. Alas., most of the Yukon and the interior of BC. It is rarely found e. of the Mackenzie River in our area, except in the far north.

OEDER'S LOUSEWORT

Pedicularis oederi M. Vahl

Smooth, thick stems, up to 20 cm (8 in.) tall, are usually solitary. Leaves, mostly basal, reduced upward, are pinnately lobed. A dense spike bears a few to many showy flowers. The calyx has triangular lanceolate teeth; the corolla is bright yellow except for the dark, brownish-red top of the galea. Found in damp alpine tundra, its range extends through most of Alas. into w. and n. Yukon and into the n. Richardson Mtns. in the Dist. of Mackenzie. It is also found in disjunct alpine locations in the Rockies.

SUDETEN LOUSEWORT

Pedicularis sudetica Willd.

Stems may be single or clustered, arising from a stout rootstock. Basal leaves are smooth, long-petioled and pinnately lobed, each segment pinnatifid to dentate; these are reduced up the stem. The inflorescence, capitate at first, elongating with age, is white and woolly. The calyx teeth are triangular; the corolla, a dark reddish-purple, has the galea longer than the tube with two prominent teeth near the apex, and the lower lip three-lobed. Occurring on rather wet, calcareous tundra and lake shores, it is circumpolar in range, common throughout much of our area except around Great Slave Lake. The young shoots are eaten boiled in soup in Siberia, according to Hultén.

WHORLED LOUSEWORT
Pedicularis verticillata L.

The stems, a few to 25 or more, rising from a branching taproot are unbranched and up to 15 cm (6 in.) tall. Leaves are both basal and on the stem; those on the stem as well as the inflorescence are borne in whorls. Purple flowers are borne in dense spikes that elongate with age. The galea is slightly arched and has no teeth; the three-cleft lower lip is longer than the galea. Found in moist meadows and on lake shores, this handsome species ranges through Alas., into the western part of the Yukon, n. to the mountains w. of the Mackenzie delta and s. into n.w. BC.

GORMAN'S PENSTEMON
Penstemon gormanii Greene

One to several tufted stems, up to 40 cm (16 in.) tall, arise from a taproot. The leaves are glabrous; the basal ones spatulate to oblong and petiolate, those on the stem linear and sessile. The 2 cm (3/4 in.)-long corolla varies considerably in colour from violet to bluish-purple; it has rounded lobes and is hairy on the inside. This attractive species is native only to the s.w. Yukon and adjacent areas, extending to west-central Alas. and barely reaching the interior of n. BC. It is locally quite common in dry gravelly and sandy areas, up to at least 900 m (3,000 ft.) in the mountains.

SMALL-FLOWERED PENSTEMON, TALL PENSTEMON

Penstemon procerus Dougl.

Slender erect stems that are rarely over 30 cm (12 in.) tall rise singly or several together from a branching rhizome. Deep green leaves in basal rosettes have long petioles about the same length as the sharply ovate blades; there are a few slender stem leaves without petioles. The leaves are glabrous or nearly so. The flowers, about 1 cm (3/8 in.) long, are deep blue and arranged in whorls in an interrupted, spike-like inflorescence. Found on dry slopes and in open forests, sandy river terraces or subalpine meadows, it ranges from s.w. Yukon, s. through the interior of BC and along the Rockies.

KITTEN TAILS

Synthyris borealis Pennell

A tufted plant rises from a short, thick, freely branching rhizome. Basal leaves

are petioled; the kidney- to heart-shaped blade is glabrous except for the ciliate margins that are deeply crenate-dentate. Flowering stems, up to 20 cm (8 in.) tall, have two or three pairs of small sessile leaves. The inflorescence is a dense spike that elongates with age; small, deep blue flowers are interspersed with hairy dentate bracts. The blue corolla has lobes as long as the tube, and the upper lip longer than the three-cleft lower lip. Stamens and style are exserted beyond the corolla. This attractive alpine is native only to c. Alas. and w. Yukon, extending through the Ogilvie to the Richardson Mtns.

BROOKLIME, AMERICAN SPEEDWELL
Veronica americana Schwein.

A glabrous, rather lax perennial, its stems are as much as 1 m (3 ft.) long, but usually less than 38 cm (15 in.). All the leaves have short petioles, and are oblong or ovate, blunt-tipped, but slightly to sharply saw-edged. The flowers are borne on racemes that arise from the axils of the upper leaves. About 6 mm (1/4 in.) wide, they are violet to lilac, and have a yellowish throat. The lowermost corolla lobe is much smaller than the other three. This attractive plant of stream banks and wet places is widespread throughout N. Amer.; it occurs in s. Yukon, n. BC, and s. Mackenzie Mtns.

SKULLCAP SPEEDWELL
Veronica scutellata L.

This plant has a weak, ascending stem that may be up to 60 cm (24 in.) long with many, linear, lanceolate leaves. Small, pale blue to white flowers in slender, lax racemes are borne in the leaf axils. It may be found on the edges of lakes, in swamps and wet places generally through s. Yukon and BC, and the s. Dist. of Mackenzie, especially around Great Slave Lake.

ALPINE SPEEDWELL
Veronica wormskjoldii Roem. & Schult.
This is a variable, perennial mountain species with notably hairy stems and leaves; the calyx and flower pedicels are sticky-glandular. Stems are unbranched and erect, up to 30 cm (12 in.) tall. The leaves are in pairs up the stem. The corolla is about 1 cm (3/8 in.) wide, dark purplish-blue with darker lines, with the upper lobe wider than the other three. It is found in meadows and on mountain slopes through our area except in the extreme north, and it barely enters the Dist. of Mackenzie in the c. Mackenzie Mtns.

OROBANCHACEAE Broom-rape Family

GROUND CONE, POQUE, BROOM-RAPE
Boschniakia rossica (Cham. & Schlecht.) Fedtsch.
This unusual plant should present no difficulty in identification. Having no green foliage, it is unable to manufacture its own food by photosynthesis. It therefore parasitizes the roots of woody plants, such as spruce and alder, and its distribution is governed by that of its host. The brownish, club-like stems rise singly or a few together from a short thick base, which attaches to the host. The flowers, in a dense terminal spike, are each in the axil of a brown, scale-like leaf. Corollas are brownish-red. It ranges through most of Alas. and the Yukon, extreme n. BC, and e. past the Mackenzie River valley to Great Bear and Great Slave lakes.

LENTIBULARIACEAE
Bladderwort Family

HAIRY BUTTERWORT
Pinguicula villosa L.

A more delicate species than *P. vulgaris* (which see), this has basal leaves no more than 1 cm (3/8 in.) long. Solitary stems, less than 10 cm (4 in.) tall, are covered in long hairs. The bluish-violet flowers are barely 1 cm long, including the spur. This tiny, rather rare, plant is circumpolar in range, and it may be found in peat bogs and around ponds in scattered locations throughout our area.

BUTTERWORT
Pinguicula vulgaris L.

The flat rosette of yellowish-green, fleshy leaves, 2.5–6 cm (1–2 1/2 in.) long with short petioles, may be found amongst mosses. The upper surfaces of the oblanceolate leaves are covered with a sticky slime for catching and digesting small insects, to supplement the diet of this semi-carnivorous plant. Violet-purple blossoms appear singly on slender 5–15 cm (2–6 in.) stems. The mouth of the corolla tube is strongly flared and five-lobed, the lower lobe being the longest and widest. The base has a long, pointed, nectar-filled spur. This is a plant of damp places by ponds, bogs or seepages. Circumpolar, it ranges throughout our area.

RUBIACEAE Madder Family

NORTHERN BEDSTRAW
Galium boreale L.

Each of the many 20–60 cm (8–24 in.)-tall, smooth, square stems of this perennial is ringed at intervals with whorls of four smooth to short-haired, three-veined leaves. Numerous white flowers, in showy terminal inflorescences, have four-lobed corollas. This is quite a common plant over most of our area except in the extreme north, or e. of Great Bear and Great Slave lakes. It is found on stony slopes, meadows, gravelly places and roadsides. Another species of bedstraw, SMALL BEDSTRAW, *G. trifidum* L., is found in wet places in the same range as the former in our area. It has a weak, slender, branched stem, with one to three white flowers on slender, arched pedicels.

CAPRIFOLIACEAE Honeysuckle Family

RED ELDERBERRY
Sambucus racemosa L.
Syn. *S. pubens* Michx.

This attractive shrub, 1–2 m (3–6 ft.) high, has fast-growing, pith-filled stems, with very large, pinnately compound leaves. Each leaf has a terminal leaflet and three to seven pairs of opposite, sharp-pointed and sawtooth-edged leaflets. Rounded clusters of creamy white, fragrant blooms are followed by bright scarlet berries. This species is found in moist areas on the edges of woods, roadsides and on grassy slopes along the coast from Alas. s. It is common in parts of the region of BC between the Alaska Panhandle and the Yukon border.

TWIN-FLOWER

Linnaea borealis L.

This very attractive small plant has long runners that creep over the forest floor. Small, leathery and broadly ovate to roundish leaves are borne in pairs along these horizontal stems. At frequent intervals, 5–10 cm (2–4 in.) flowering stems are produced, forking at the top to support two slender, trumpet-shaped flowers that are rose pink and sweet-scented. Circumboreal in range in its various forms, it is common through most of our area in mossy open woodland or in thickets. This plant was a favourite of the 18th-century Swedish botanist, Linnaeus, the orginator of modern biological nomenclature, and its name commemorates him.

HIGH-BUSH CRANBERRY
Viburnum edule (Michx.) Raf.
This is a common, erect to straggling, oppo-
site-leaved, 1/2–2 m (1 1/2–6 ft.)-tall shrub.
Mature leaves are rounded in outline, with two
pronounced notches at the outer end, and are
further sharply serrate. Younger leaves are
pointed-lanceolate and, like the others, short-
hairy beneath, especially along the larger veins.
Flowers are greenish-white and tubular,
arranged in flattened clusters between pairs of
leaves along the stem, rather than at the end of
the branches. Flower parts are in fives, with
very short stamens not projecting beyond the
mouth of the wide, five-lobed corolla tube.
The flowers are followed by brilliantly scarlet
fruit in the fall, when the leaves turn a vivid
crimson-purple. It occurs in cold, damp woods
and semi-open woodland margins of lakes and
streams throughout our area, but on the n. coast
only in the Mackenzie delta.

VALERIANACEAE Valerian Family

CAPITATE VALERIAN, MOUNTAIN HELIOTROPE
Valeriana capitata Pall.
This species is easily distinguishable from *V. sitchensis* (which see) by the upper
stem leaves, which are sessile. Single stems, up to 1 m (3 ft.) tall, bear a densely
capitate inflorescence of pinkish flowers that fade to white, subtended by three
large three-lobed bracts. Found in moist mountain meadows, tundra and river
flats, it ranges throughout Alas. and the Yukon, reaching the Mackenzie delta
and the east slopes of the Richardson and Mackenzie Mtns.

SITKA VALERIAN
Valeriana sitchensis Bong.
Succulent stems, square in cross-section, may be up to 75 cm (30 in.) tall.
Generally glabrous leaves appear in opposite pairs up the stem on long petioles
that become progressively shorter. The leaves are pinnately cleft, the terminal
lobe larger than the one to four lateral pairs. All have slightly serrate edges.
Flowers are clustered in a flat-topped arrangement; they are pink at first, fading
to white, and strongly scented. This is an attractive plant of moist, shaded thickets and rocky slopes, ranging from c. Yukon s., and e. to the Mackenzie Mtns.
NORTHERN VALERIAN, *V. septrionalis* Rydb. (Syn. *V. dioica* L.), found in
moist places throughout s. Yukon and n. BC, is a smaller plant. It has a distinctive cluster of entire-margined, oblong to ovate, long-petioled basal leaves and
the inflorescence, lightly compact, has white flowers.

CAMPANULACEAE Bluebell Family

ALPINE HAREBELL
Campanula lasiocarpa Cham.
A single flower is borne at the top of a 5–10 cm (2–4 in.) leafy stem that rises
from a creeping rhizome. The white-hairy calyx has linear lobes, each with one
or two pairs of thread-like teeth.
The corolla, 2–2.5 cm (3/4–1 in.)
long, is bell-shaped and deep lilac
blue. *Lasiocarpa* means "fuzzy
fruit" (a reference to the pubescent capsule). It is found in alpine
meadows and sandy tundra up to
at least 1,600 m (5,500 ft.) in the
mountains through most of Alas.,
and from c. Yukon s. into n. BC
and e. to the eastern slopes of the
Mackenzie Mtns.

YUKON BELLFLOWER

Campanula aurita Greene

One to several straight, slender stems, 10–30 cm (4–12 in.) tall, arise from a branching rootstock. Only stem leaves are present; these are glabrous and lanceolate. Flowers are solitary, or a few, at the top of the stem. The deep blue corolla is cleft nearly to the base; the reflexed lobes are lanceolate, surpassing the calyx lobes. Found in turfy or gravelly places on cal-careous soil, it occurs only in the interior and alpine parts of Alas., c. Yukon, the west-central Dist. of Mackenzie and n. BC.

HAREBELL, BLUEBELL

Campanula rotundifolia L.

Slender, erect or ascending 10–25 cm (4–10 in.)-high, leafy stems, from freely branching rhizomes, are often numerous, forming dense mats. The specific name, when one considers the slender and sessile linear leaves of the stem, may appear inappropriate, but the blades of the basal leaves (which may wither early) are indeed round in outline. They are slightly to strongly toothed, and

have petioles two to three times as long as the blades. The large purple-blue flowers are broadly bell-like, 1–2 cm (3/8–3/4 in.) in diame-ter, usually solitary but sometimes several together. Circumboreal in range, harebell reaches into n.w. BC and the Yukon s. of Whitehorse. It may also be found on the Canol Road, in the upper Mackenzie River valley and on the e. side of Great Slave Lake.

ARCTIC HAREBELL
Campanula uniflora L.

A thick taproot gives rise to one or a few unbranched stems up to 30 cm (12 in.) high that are rather stout, smooth and often decumbent at the base. The leaves are smooth, quite leathery, dark green and linear-lanceolate. Solitary, slightly nodding flowers become erect in fruit. The narrow, pale blue corolla is slightly larger than the calyx lobes. This small, attractive plant may be found on dry, stony, calcareous ridges and screes. High Arctic–alpine, its range is scattered from the coast of the Bering Strait e. across n. Canada. It is found through n. Alas. and the Yukon on the Richardson Mtns. and also in s.w. Yukon.

KALM'S LOBELIA
Lobelia kalmii L.

Simple or branched stems up to about 20 cm (8 in.) tall have a basal rosette of spatulate-obovate, pubescent, purplish leaves. The narrowly oblanceolate stem leaves are alternate. Showy, pale lavender-mauve flowers with a white "eye," borne in a few-flowered raceme, have an irregular corolla, inverted so that what is technically the three-lobed upper lip appears on the lower edge of the tube. This species of moist, calcareous meadows and pond margins appears in our area around Liard Hotsprings and in other locations in the upper Mackenzie River drainage system and w. of Great Slave Lake. Lobelia is named for Matthias de L'Obel, an early French physician who became botanist to James I.

ASTERACEAE
Sunflower Family

COMMON YARROW, MILFOIL
Achillea millefolium L.
Syn. *A. borealis* Bong.

An aromatic, medicinal oil was formerly extracted from this plant. Yarrow grows from a slender, freely branching rhizome with erect, simple or branching stems up to 30 cm (12 in.) or even 60 cm (24 in.) high. The leaves are three or four times pinnately compound, having a "ferny" appearance. The plant is topped by a flat cluster of small white (sometimes pinkish) flowers, blooming till late summer. It is common in some parts of our area, especially in the south on roadsides and open gravelly or sandy places.

SIBERIAN YARROW
Achillea sibirica Ledeb.

Stems, usually branching high up, may be up to 80 cm (32 in.) tall, either single or several together from a branching rootstock. The lanceolate leaves, 5–10 cm (2–4 in.) long, are sessile and sharply toothed, not compound as in *A. millefolium* (which see). The many heads are 5–8 mm (3/16–5/16 in.) in diameter; the ray flowers are white, three-toothed at the tip. This may be found on rocky river banks and lake shores and in meadows across c. Alas. to w. Yukon, along the Mackenzie River and in n.e. BC.

PEARLY EVERLASTING
Anaphalis margaritacea (L.)
Benth. & Hook.

This is a highly variable species. It grows up to 30 or even 60 cm (12–24 in.) tall from a perennial rhizome. The stem is erect, unbranched and densely white-woolly, as are the undersides of the numerous, sessile, 5–10 cm (2–4 in.), linear-lanceolate leaves that alternate up its length. The flower heads are crowded in a flattened cluster; each tiny yellow floret is closely surrounded by pale, papery bracts. The name "everlasting" comes from the fact that these plants are often dried for winter ornamentation. They do not usually bloom until July, but the flowers may last into the first snow of winter. It may be found on roadsides and open forests in the Alaska Panhandle and n.w. BC. It has been found in in the Mackenzie Mtns. and s.e. Yukon.

SINGLE-HEADED PUSSY-TOES
Antennaria monocephala DC.

This is a tiny plant, often forming small mats, with erect shoots. Basal leaves are linear-oblanceolate and stem leaves linear, both with flat, brown, papery tips about 2 mm (1/16 in.) long; the leaves are not more than 1 cm (3/8 in.) in length and thinly woolly. Solitary flower heads top stems about 5 cm (2 in.) high, but sometimes up to 15 cm (6 in.). The involucral bracts are green at the base, dark brown in the middle and olive green to golden brown towards the slender, tapering tips. The styles are conspicuously exserted well beyond the tubes of the florets. A common species above timberline of granitic mountains in snow-patch vegetation, ravines and avalanche paths, it ranges through most of the Yukon and Alas., e. to the Mackenzie Mtns., and in isolated locations in the high mountains of n. BC.

SHOWY EVERLASTING

Antennaria pulcherrima (Hook.) Greene
Solitary, leafy stems, 20–50 cm (8–20 in.)
tall, arise from a branching rhizome. Basal
leaves, up to 12 cm (4 3/4 in.) long and 14
mm (7/16 in.) broad, are oblanceolate, acute,
long-petioled, prominently three-veined and
grey-silvery tomentose on both surfaces; the
lower stem leaves are the same. The inflorescence is a compact cyme with 4–12 heads,
two or three on each branch. The pistillate
heads are large, 6 mm (1/4 in.) high; the staminate ones are smaller. Often found in
large clumps on river flats, meadows and
alpine slopes, up to at least 1,100 m (3,600

ft.), it ranges through c. Alas., c. and s. Yukon and s. through BC. Approximately
20 species of the genus *Antennaria* occur in our area. Many of these are variable
and superficially similar, so three of the most distinct species have been illustrated and described.

PINK PUSSY-TOES

Antennaria rosea Greene
A mat-forming plant, it spreads with long,
strongly developed, freely branching stolons, each
ending in an erect or ascending leafy rosette that
produces a flowering stem the following year.
Basal leaves, about 2 cm (3/4 in.) long, are
oblanceolate and acute. The flowering stems,
10–30 cm (4–12 in.) high, have 8–10 linear, 2 cm-
long leaves tapering to a thin point. The inflorescence is rather compact, with
three to five small heads in a hemispherical cyme. Involucres are about 5 mm
(3/16 in.) high, the membranous tips of the bracts bright to pale pink, a distinguishing feature of the species. The pap-
pus is dirty white and not glossy.
Staminate plants are unknown in our
area. Pink pussy-toes may be found in
sandy places, open woods and flood
plains, up to about 1,800 m (6,000 ft.) in
the mountains; it ranges from s. and c.
Alas., e. through most of the Yukon
except the far north, in the Dist. of
Mackenzie in the upper Mackenzie River
system, around Great Slave Lake, and s.
through BC.

ALPINE ARNICA

Arnica angustifolia Vahl
Syn. *A. alpina* (L.) Olin

A variable, tufted plant, it has a rosette of lanceolate, petioled leaves and a single stem 20–30 cm (8–12 in.) high (in some forms up to 50 cm (20 in.)). There are one or two pairs of linear, sessile leaves and one large head; sometimes, in taller forms, two smaller lateral heads (rarely four) occur in the axils of the uppermost leaves. The ray and disc flowers are bright yellow. Found in dry, sandy, gravelly places and grassy open forests, it ranges in a variety of forms throughout our area. A smaller, extremely hairy form of alpine arnica may be found in scattered alpine–arctic locations.

HEART-LEAVED ARNICA

Arnica cordifolia Hook.

Stems are usually single, or a few together, reaching 40–50 cm (16–20 in.) in height from a branching rhizome. There are usually three or four pairs of stem

leaves, the lower ones with cordate and shallowly serrate blades on slender petioles as long as the blades, the upper ones progressively smaller and nearly sessile. There are one to three flower heads, the terminal one occasionally as much as 5 cm (2 in.) in diameter. The pappus is white, or nearly so, with very small, barb-like projections. Found in open forests and alpine meadows, it ranges through west-central and s.w. Yukon, e. to the east slope of the Mackenzie Mtns., s.e. through BC, and along the Rockies.

LAKE LOUISE ARNICA

Arnica frigida C.A. Meyer

Single stems, 10–30 cm (4–12 in.) tall, arise from an ascending, branched and black-scaly rhizome. The leaves, mainly basal, have oblanceolate or obovate blades 3–6 mm (1/8–1/4 in.) long, narrowing to a short, winged petiole. They are sparingly pubescent or glabrate, and the margins may be slightly dentate. The stem leaves are narrower, entire and sessile. Flower heads are usually solitary, nodding when young. The ray and disc flowers are pale yellow. Referred to by many authors as a subspecies of *A. louiseana* Farr., this species is extremely variable in pubescence and leaf form. Found on dry stony slopes throughout most of Alas. and the Yukon, it ranges e. to the eastern slopes of the Mackenzie Mtns. and to the Mackenzie delta region. There are about nine species of the genus *Arnica* commonly or rarely found in our area, most of which have superficially rather similar showy, yellow flowers. The descriptions and illustrations of four representative and quite commonly encountered species are included.

LESSING'S ARNICA

Arnica lessingii (Torr. & Gray) Greene

Soliary stems, up to 25 cm (10 in.) tall, rise from a rosette of oblanceolate basal leaves with finely serrulate margins. The single heads are always nodding, a distinct recognition feature of this species. In alpine and sub-alpine meadows this may be found throughout most of Alas., the Yukon and n. BC, reaching the eastern slopes of the Richardson and Mackenzie Mtns. The lotion "Arnica," used extensively in medicine, is an extract from the European species, MOUNTAIN TOBACCO, *A. montana* L.

ALASKA WORMWOOD
Artemisia alaskana Rydb.
Simple, ascending stems, up to 40 cm (16 in.) tall, arise from a stout, many-headed taproot. Leaves, in a basal rosette and up the stem, are fan-shaped and pinnate with five divisions, each division cleft into oblong to linear blunt sections. Stem and leaves are light grey-tomentose. The nodding flower heads are mostly solitary on slender peduncles, the uppermost sessile. Occurring on gravel bars, rocky ledges in calcareous cliffs, and screes up to about 1,800 m (6,000 ft.), it is found in alpine parts of Alas., throughout most of the Yukon, extending into the Dist. of Mackenzie in the Richardson Mtns. and in n.w. BC. PRAIRIE SAGEWORT, *A. frigida* Willd., is another sagewort (or wormwood) found in our area, and one of the most fragrant species of this group. Its graceful stems, less than 40 cm (16 in.) tall, have scattered, feathery and fragrant foliage. The leaves are strikingly silvery-silky, two or three times ternately divided into many narrow divisions. The small flower heads are pale yellow. This is a plant of dry, open slopes, rocky places and prairies, up to about 900 m (3,000 ft.) in the mountains. It is widespread, ranging through c. Alas. and the Yukon (except for the far north), and s. through the interior of BC. It also occurs in the Mackenzie delta, in the upper Mackenzie drainage system, and on the n.w. coast of the Dist. of Mackenzie.

ARCTIC WORMWOOD
Artemisia arctica Less.
Each plant has one to a few stems, up to 50 cm (20 in.) or more tall, which are usually glabrous and often reddish or purplish, rarely hairy. Leaves of the basal rosette have long, slender petioles, as long as the twice to three times pinnately divided blade. Flower heads are mostly solitary and nodding. The ovate to elliptical involucral bracts, 5 mm (3/16 in.) both long and broad, have thin, transparent, black margins that strongly contrast with the narrower green centre. Flowers are yellow. Arctic wormwood may be found in moist alpine meadows to at least 1,800 m (6,000 ft.) throughout our area, ranging e. to the east slopes of the Mackenzie and Richardson Mtns. and s. through BC.

NORTHERN WORMWOOD
Artemisia borealis Pall.

This highly variable, tufty plant often bears many simple or branched stems up to 30 cm (12 in.) tall, and many basal leaves, bipinnate with linear lobes, borne on long slender petioles. Inflorescences are extended; the globular flower heads, 3–4 mm (1/8 in.) in diameter, are supported by linear bracts, the lower of which are two- and three-lobed. It is found on dry sandy slopes by sea or lake shores or on river banks. Circumboreal, it ranges through c. and n. Alas., s. Yukon and n. BC, extending s. along the Rockies. It also occurs on the n. coast of the Dist. of Mackenzie and around Great Bear and Great Slave lakes.

PURPLE WORMWOOD

Artemisia globularia Bess.

This is a tufted, dwarf, grey-pubescent species. The basal leaves, once or twice divided into three lobes, are crowded. A short stem, not more than 5 cm (2 in.) high, bears a globular inflorescence consisting of five to eight dark purple to blackish heads. The involucral bracts are brown with black margins. Found on gravelly alpine slopes, it appears in the British Mtns. of n. Yukon, and it may yet be found in the Richardson Mtns.

MOUNTAIN WORMWOOD
Artemisia tilesii Ledeb.

This species is readily distinguished from the other wormwoods by its foliage which, however, is quite variable. Large, pinnately lobed green leaves, the upper ones linear, are smooth above and grey-woolly beneath. They are borne on freely branched stems up to 50 cm (20 in.) tall. Small, somewhat nodding flower heads are borne in a spike-like inflorescence. The involucral bracts have broad, dark margins. Growing in sandy places up to 1,800 m (6,000 ft.) in mountains, and throughout our area n. of 60° N.L., this plant is highly variable and local forms may be found.

MOUNTAIN ASTER
Aster alpinus L. ssp. *vierhapperi* Onno

A small, compact plant, it has a tuft of numerous, oblanceolate and blunt-ended basal leaves up to 6 cm (2 3/8 in.) long, and smaller, linear leaves up the 10–15 cm (4–6 in.)-tall stem. The leaves and stem are rough with stiff, spreading hairs. Flower heads are terminal and solitary, about 2.5 cm (1 in.) in diameter. The rays are lavender, bluish or white. Mountain aster occurs on dry grassy slopes and alpine tundra through most of the Yukon to the east slope of the Richardson Mtns., east of the Mackenzie delta and along the Mackenzie valley to the w. shores of Great Bear and Great Slave lakes, and in n.e. BC.

SIBERIAN ASTER

Aster sibiricus L.

Usually several leafy stems, up to 30 cm (12 in.) tall, arise from a branching rhizome. The leaves are very variable, but they are generally lanceolate to oblanceolate, sessile or short-petioled, usually with serrate margins, glabrous above and hairy beneath. Flower heads, solitary or a few, have purple ray flowers, and the pappus is reddish-brown or yellowish. A plant of gravelly river flats, dry meadows or open forests, it is common throughout our area.

DOUGLAS ASTER

Aster subspicatus Nees

This is a tall plant; the many slim, leafy stems are often over 1 m (3 ft.) tall. The leaves are entire to slightly toothed, oblanceolate below but becoming lanceolate upward. Lower leaves often wither early; they generally have short petioles that disappear upward, most upper leaves being sessile. Flower heads are about 2.5 cm (1 in.) broad with purple to rosy-purple rays. Disc flowers are yellowish to reddish. This aster is very variable and is widespread in coastal regions from Alas. to Cal. It may be found on stream banks and roadsides, and in open woods in extreme n.w. BC; it has also been reported in the Cassiar Mtns. near the BC–Yukon border. The three asters described here are perhaps the ones most likely be be encountered, but there are at least another 10 species that occur in scattered locations in various regions of our area.

CHRYSANTHEMUM
Chrysanthemum integrifolium
Richards.

This is a tufted, dwarf, perennial plant with single or many leafless flower stems bearing solitary heads. The leaves are 2 cm (3/4 in.) long and are linear. Flowering stems, up to 10 cm (4 in.) tall, woolly above, have one or more reduced leafy bracts. Flowers, about 1.5 cm (5/8 in.) in diameter, have white, three-toothed ray flowers and yellow disc flowers. This is an Arctic–alpine plant of rocky, calcareous slopes. It ranges

across northern Alas., n. Yukon and the Dist. of Mackenzie n. of Great Bear Lake, extending s. on the western side of the Mackenzie River into the upper Mackenzie drainage system in n. BC.

ELEGANT HAWK'S-BEARD
Crepis elegans Hook.

This is a dwarf perennial growing from a many-headed taproot. Basal leaves, up to 7 cm (2 3/4 in.) long, usually entire, with the oval blade tapering to a narrow petiole, are purplish-green and glabrous; the stem leaves reduced and narrow.

Flowering stems, up to about 20 cm (8 in.) tall, are branched above the middle. The small cylindrical heads in terminal clusters of two to five, have yellow or pale purple ligules; the pappus is white. Occurring on river banks, flood plains, gravel bars and lake shores, it is locally common in e. Alas., throughout the Yukon, e. to Great Bear and Great Slave lakes, and s. through the interior of BC.

DWARF HAWK'S-BEARD
Crepis nana Richards.

A dense mass of cylindrical yellow flower heads and long-petioled, elliptical to oblanceolate, sometimes toothed leaves forms a rounded, cushion-like tuft about 5 cm (2 in.) high. The leaves, often exceeding the flower heads, are glabrous. Rays are yellow or purplish, the pappus white. Found on calcareous slopes and rather dry, gravelly places throughout the Yukon and n. BC, it extends e. to the eastern slopes of the Mackenzie and Richardson Mtns. and the Coppermine region. It is found in much of Alas. except the Yukon River basin and the s. coast.

FLEABANE DAISY
Erigeron acris L.

Smooth, leafy flower stems of this highly variable species may be 30–80 cm (12–32 in.) tall. Basal leaves are oblanceolate, tapering to a narrow, petiole-like base; the stem leaves are lanceolate and sessile. Mature heads when expanded may be up to 2 cm (3/4 in.) in diameter, the involucral bracts linear and the ligules pale pink to lilac. There is a ring of tubular pistillate flowers between the marginal ligulate and the central "perfect" flowers. The pappus is large and reddish-brown. Occurring in open spruce forests, on sandy river banks and on lake shores, it is circumpolar, ranging through most of Alas. and throughout our area. Another species, *E. elatus* (Hook.) Greene, is found throughout s. Yukon in open, boggy woods. A more slender plant, it has fewer or solitary heads that are borne on erect, hairy peduncles. Yet another, SPEAR-LEAF FLEABANE, *E. lonchophyllus* Hook., is hairy, with leaves that are much narrower, and ligules that are inconspicuous. This is a widespread species.

TUFTED FLEABANE
Erigeron caespitosus Nutt.

As the name *caespitosus* (tufted) implies, this is a tufted plant arising from a stout taproot, with usually many ascending leafy stems up to 15 cm (6 in.) long. Basal leaves are narrowly oblanceolate, stem leaves linear and reduced upwards. Flower heads, solitary or a few per stem, are 1.5–2.5 cm (5/8–1 in.) in diameter, the ligules creamy white or pinkish, much longer than the involucral bracts. Tufted fleabane is found in dry rocky or sandy places in e. Alas., and in w. and s.w. Yukon.

CUTLEAF FLEABANE
Erigeron compositus Pursh
This densely tufted plant has many crowded basal leaves that are two to four times ternately lobed into linear segments. The flowering stems, up to 15 cm (6 in.) tall, are leafless, except for possibly a few reduced bracts. Solitary heads have rays that are white or pale lilac, though lacking in some forms, May–early June. It is found in dry rocky or gravelly places throughout most of our area.

MOUNTAIN FLEABANE
Erigeron humilis Grah.
This is a small, densely hairy plant. Single, or several, erect stems with dense greyish hairs rise from a basal cluster of spatulate leaves that are reduced up the stem to about 2 cm (3/4 in.) long. Solitary heads have many narrow, white ligules about 6 mm (1/4 in.) long that age to bluish-violet. Disc flowers are yellow. It grows in moist, grassy places, often below snow banks, throughout most of our area.

COASTAL FLEABANE, ASTER FLEABANE, MOUNTAIN DAISY

Erigeron peregrinus (Pursh) Greene
A variable species, it has, generally, single, unbranched, very leafy
stems up to 50 cm (20 in.) tall.
The leaves are oblanceolate to
spatulate, smooth or somewhat
villous and ciliate in the margins,
reduced in size upwards. Solitary
flower heads have white, pink,
purplish or blue ligules. The pappus is tawny. It is found in grassy
meadows primarily in the Coast
Mtns. but extends into n.w. BC,
the extreme s.w. Yukon, and
throughout coastal areas in s. Alas.

ARCTIC FLEABANE

Erigeron purpuratus Greene
A dwarf, loosely matted perennial, it has a cluster of oblanceolate basal leaves,
usually with entire margins, about 2.5 cm (1 in.) long. Solitary heads, about 1.5
cm (5/8 in.) in diameter, are borne on slender, hairy stems that are up to 6 cm
(2 3/8 in.) high. Pointed involucral bracts have purplish hairs. The ligules are
white when young, turning purplish with age. This plant, of open gravelly
places, is native only to parts of e. and n. Alas. and of w. and s.w. Yukon, n.w. BC
and the Mackenzie Mtns.

HAPLOPAPPUS
Haplopappus macleanii
Brandegee

Large mats, up to 1 m (3 ft.) in diameter, may be formed. The distinct foliage has smooth, linear, rigid leaves crowded at the ends of more or less woody branches. Flowering stems, leafy below, bear solitary heads. Ray and disc flowers are bright yellow. This handsome plant grows only in the upper Yukon River basin, on rather dry, open, stony slopes. The picture was taken in early July in Lapie Canyon.

NARROW-LEAVED HAWKWEED
Hieracium scabriusculum Schwein.

Smooth, stiffly erect stems may reach 1 m (3 ft.) or more in height. Lanceolate or oblong leaves, rather stiff and firm, have entire or (occasionally) sparsely toothed margins. The few to many heads have bright yellow ligules. In moist woodland clearings or roadsides, this plant may be found in s.e. Yukon and n. BC.

ARCTIC SWEET COLTSFOOT
Petasites frigidus (L.) Fries

Simple stems, up to 50 cm (20 in.) high, from creeping rootstocks, develop before the more or less triangular, rather coarsely toothed and deeply lobed leaves. Their upper surface is deep green, the lower densely white-woolly. Flowers are more or less white or pink to purplish. Found in moist sandy places by lake shores and stream banks, it ranges throughout Alas., extending e. to Great Bear Lake, and along the coast of the Dist. of Mackenzie. Another species, ARROW-LEAVED SWEET COLTS-FOOT, *P. sagittatus* (Banks) Gray, differs from the above in that the leaves, up to 30 cm (12 in.) long and 25 cm (10 in.) broad, are arrow-shaped, and the flowers are borne in a more flat-topped cluster. This is found in very wet places, often standing in water, in scattered locations throughout our area.

COLTSFOOT
Petasites palmatus (Ait.) Gray

The stem appears through the ground soon
after the snow has melted. The shoot bears
many flower heads in a flattened cluster. Ray
flowers, few and short, are usually white. Soon
after the appearance of the flowering stems,
stout leaf shoots emerge. By the time the
flower shoots have withered, the fan-like leaves
have reached their full size, 30 cm (12 in.) or
more wide. They are white-haired below,
deeply five- to seven-lobed at least half their
width (the lobes further toothed), and borne
on strong petioles about 50–60 cm (20–24 in.)
long. The flower stems arise from different

points on the creeping rhizome than do the leaves, and at different times, so it is
possible not to associate them with one another. This species ranges in swampy
places from s. Yukon and the Peel watershed in the n.e., and s. through the
interior of BC.

SAUSSUREA
Saussurea angustifolia (Willd.) DC.

Dark purple, smooth or floccose stems, up to 30 cm (12 in.) tall, arise from a
creeping rhizome. There are no basal leaves. Stem leaves are smooth or floccose

beneath, and linear to lanceolate, the
lower ones 5–10 cm (2–4 in.) long,
becoming reduced upwards. Three to five
discoid purple flower heads are arranged
in a terminal corymb. Involucral bracts
are in three or four rows, and the plumose
pappus is tawny. Occurring in dry places
in tundra, it ranges through all of Alas.
except the s. coast and the Panhandle,
extending e. through n. and c. Yukon to
the Mackenzie River and around Great
Bear Lake to the n.e. Dist. of Mackenzie.
Another species, STICKY SAUSSUREA, *S.
viscida* Hult., which is regarded by some
authors as a variety of *S. angustifolia*, is a
smaller plant, not more than 10 cm (4 in.)

tall with leaves that are not floccose. Yet another species, AMERICAN SAW-
WORT, *S. americana* DC., often over 1 m (3 ft.) tall, with lanceolate-ovate,
coarsely toothed leaves that are pale beneath and floccose when young, may be
found in the Coast Mtns. of n.w. BC, and s.w. Yukon.

GROUNDSEL, DARK PURPLE RAGWORT

Senecio atropurpureus (Ledeb.) Fedtsch.
Syn. *S. frigidus* (Richards.) Less.

Single stems, up to 20 cm (8 in.) high, bear up to six sessile, ovate-oblanceolate, slightly fleshy leaves. Basal leaves are petiolate with blades up to 2 cm (3/4 in.) long. Leaves are always alternate in the genus *Senecio* so it can easily be distinguished from the arnicas, where they are always arranged in opposite pairs. Heads are solitary with yellow disc and ray flowers. In moist tundra it may be found throughout much of the Yukon, in the Mackenzie River valley, and in the n. regions of the Dist. of Mackenzie.

MASTODON FLOWER, MARSH FLEABANE

Senecio congestus (R. Br.) DC.

A stout, hollow, densely hirsute, simple stem reaches 1 m (3 ft.) tall, though it is sometimes shorter and more slender. The numerous leaves are sessile, linear-oblong and sinuate-toothed. Numerous small flower heads are packed into tight woolly clusters. Ligules are short and yellow, pappus long and white. A locally common plant of wet places and disturbed areas, it is circumpolar, extending through Alas. (except on the s. coast), and through the extreme n., c. and s.w. Yukon, and most of the Dist. of Mackenzie. The young leaves and flowering stems are edible and may be used as salad.

TWICE-HAIRY BUTTERWEED
Senecio lindstroemii (Ostenf.) Pors.
Syn. *S. fuscatus* (Jord. & Fourr.) Hayek
Syn. *S. tundricola* Tolm.
The pubescence of the leaves is of two types (hence the name): coarse, flattened hairs are overlain by a mat of cobwebby hairs. Basal leaves are broadly oblance-olate to ovate and usually sessile and entire or with irregular teeth; stem leaves are reduced. Stems, solitary, are up to 25 cm (10 in.) tall. Usually single heads have linear involucral bracts that are dark purplish-tipped; ligules (sometimes absent), 2 cm (3/4 in.) long, are bright orange-yellow; disc flowers are yellow with reddish-purple lobes. Found in alpine meadows in e. and n. Alas., it extends into the c., s.w. and extreme n. Yukon, and to the east slope of the Richardson and n.e. Mackenzie Mtns.

FEW-LEAVED GROUNDSEL, ALPINE MEADOW BUTTERWEED

Senecio streptanthifolius Greene
Syn. *S. cymbalarioides* Nutt.

Single or many stems, up to 30 cm (12 in.) tall, have glabrous or floccose leaves that are more or less succulent. Basal leaves are broadly elliptical to roundish, entire or crenate towards the apex; stem leaves are few, reduced in size and pinnately lobed. Several heads are borne in open cymes. Rays, 6–12 mm (1/4–1/2 in.) long, are yellow. Found in wet places in the mountains up to at least 900 m (3,000 ft.), it ranges s. from c. Yukon through n. BC.

BLACK-TIPPED GROUNDSEL

Senecio lugens Richards.

Solitary or clustered, unbranched stems, 5–40 cm (2–16 in.) tall, arise from a stout rhizome. The oblanceolate leaves, mainly basal, taper to a narrow petiole. Flower heads, a few to a dozen or more, are in a loose corymb. The inner involucral bracts are prominently black-tipped; the ligules are yellow, up to 14 mm (9/16 in.) long, but usually much shorter. It is found through our area e. to Great Bear and Great Slave lakes, on lake shores and river banks, in meadows and open forests, often amongst willows. The black tips of the involucral bracts used to be considered by the Inuit as a sign of mourning for the massacre at Bloody Falls on the Coppermine River of a group of Inuit by a party of Natives accompanying Samuel Hearne in 1771.

RAYLESS ALPINE BUTTERWEED
Senecio pauciflorus Pursh

A perennial with glabrous stems up to 60 cm (24 in.) tall, it has somewhat fleshy leaves. The basal ones, up to 10 cm (4 in.) long, elliptic-ovate and finely toothed, are borne on long, slender petioles. Stem leaves are reduced in size, oblong and variously toothed or lobed. Flower heads, six or often more, have involucres about 1 cm (3/8 in.) long, ligules lacking, flowers orange to reddish and involucral bracts reddish to purple. A variable species, it is easily identified by its lack of ligules and bright orange flower heads. Some authors include this with RAYLESS MOUNTAIN BUTTERWEED, *S. indecorus* Greene, which has more numerous flower heads and mostly yellow flowers. It is found in wet places and on meadows, lake shores and river flats from c. Alas., through c. and s. Yukon e. to the Mackenzie Mtns., and s. through the interior of BC.

BALSAM GROUNDSEL
Senecio pauperculus Michx.

This is rather similar to *S. streptanthifolius* (which see), but the heads are usually borne in what appears at first to be an umbel-like inflorescence. The leaves are thin; the basal leaves are oblanceolate with crennate margins, stem leaves pinnate with acute segments. Stems, up to 50 cm (20 in.) tall and smooth, bear rarely more than six ligulate flower heads, the ligules being pale yellow. This may be found in wet places throughout most of our area except the n.e. Dist. of Mackenzie.

DWARF ARCTIC BUTTERWEED

Senecio cymbalaria Pursh
Syn. *S. resedifolius* Less.
A smooth, unbranched stem rises from a cluster of ovate to kidney-shaped leaves that are deeply crenate-dentate. Stem leaves are pinnately lobed, reduced upwards. Solitary heads with purplish bracts have long yellow ligules, reddish on the back (which may sometimes be lacking), and orange disc flowers. This may be found in rocky places through the n. and c. mountains of Alas., ranging e. through the extreme n. and w. Yukon, including the Richardson, Wernecke and n. Mackenzie Mtns.

SPEAR-HEAD SENECIO, ARROWLEAF SENECIO

Senecio triangularis Hook.
A tall, glabrous perennial, its often clustered stems may reach 1.5 m (4 1/2 ft.) or more tall, but are usually about 1 m (3 ft.). The species name describes the long, pointed-triangular leaves that make identification unmistakable. They occur all the way up the stems, becoming reduced from about 20 cm (8 in.) in length to about 8 cm (3 1/8 in.). Lower leaves are strikingly notched along the edges, with a squared-off base and rather long petioles, but the upper leaves have serrate margins, with a wedge-shaped base and no petiole. The flattened cluster of 2.5 cm (1 in.)-wide flower heads is quite showy. The rays number 5–12, usually eight. A locally common plant that may be abundant in wet meadows or on stream banks from c. Yukon s., it ranges e. to the east slope of the s. Mackenzie Mtns. and s. down the Rockies and along the coast.

YUKON GROUNDSEL
Senecio yukonensis Pors.

Single hairy stems, up to 30 cm (12 in.) tall, rise from clusters of oblanceolate, entire-margined, basal leaves; stem leaves are linear and reduced. Up to five densely clustered, yellowish, woolly heads have lanceolate involucral bracts that are dark green or black, and pale yellow rays. Found in mossy alpine heathland and exposed ridges, this occurs from n. and c. Alas., through most of the Yukon, e. to the Mackenzie and Richardson Mtns. and n. to the Arctic coast. Approximately 20 species of *Senecio* are known to occur in our area.

CANADA GOLDENROD
Solidago canadensis L.

This perennial grows from branched, creeping rhizomes, sending up stems that may reach 2 m (6 ft.) tall, but are usually about 1 m (3 ft.) or less. Numerous alternate leaves are lanceolate-linear, sharply saw-toothed to entire. They are

sessile and only slightly reduced in size upwards. The terminal inflorescence is a crowded panicle. Often the branchlets are slightly down-curved, with the yellow flower heads chiefly on the upper side. Most flower heads have 10–17 ray flowers. Canada goldenrod may be found in open forests and meadows, but it is most often seen along roadsides. Its occurrence is patchy in our area. It has been located in the Yukon River valley in the Dawson City area, in south-central Yukon, throughout s.e. Yukon near the BC border and in adjacent BC. It also ranges n. in the upper Mackenzie drainage system to about 66° N.L.

DUNE GOLDENROD
Solidago simplex Kunth
Syn. *S. decumbens* Greene
Syn. *S. oreophila* Rydb.

Stems 20–40 cm (8–16 in.) tall, solitary or a few together arising from an ascending rhizome, are dark purplish and nearly glabrous. Leaves, mostly basal, are oblanceolate, entire or shallow-toothed; stem leaves are lanceolate and reduced. The elongated inflorescence has numerous flower heads in a contracted, spike-like panicle, sometimes with lateral branches over 2 cm (3/4 in.) long. The yellow rays are up to 6 mm (1/4 in.) long. It may be found on gravel bars, river banks, lake shores or in open forests in e. Alas. It ranges through s. Yukon, n. BC, around Great Slave Lake and in the upper Mackenzie drainage system to near the Arctic coast.

NORTHERN GOLDENROD, MOUNTAIN GOLDENROD
Solidago multiradiata Ait.

Ascending stems, up to 40 cm (16 in.) tall, have oblanceolate to elliptical leaves with serrate margins that are villous at the base and on the petioles. The upper leaves are reduced in size and do not exceed the flowers. There are usually several flower heads in a dense, corymbiform inflorescence, the pedicels white-villous. Lanceolate involucral bracts are 20–30 in number, and the bright yellow ligules 12–18. It is often common in open forests, meadows and gravel bars throughout most of our area except the e. Dist. of Mackenzie.

HORNED DANDELION

Taraxacum ceratophorum (Ledeb.) DC.

This is one of a few species that have prominent "horns" near the tips of the involucral bracts, so that the name horned dandelion may be applied to any one of this group. Many of the dandelions reproduce by forming viable seeds without fertilization, thus giving rise to races of numerous identical plants. These closely related races are often classified as separate but very similar species, forming a taxonomically confusing group. The leaves are sharply incised, with the segments pointing backwards; the mid-rib is usually purplish. Flower heads are large and may be up to 5 cm (2 in.) in diameter in very vigorous specimens. The green bracts are prominently horned; ligules are pale yellow. Achenes, up to 6 mm (1/4 in.) long, are yellowish grey, the upper half spiny, the beak 5–8 mm (3/16–5/16 in.) long. Found in rather moist places, often in disturbed areas and near human habitation or animal burrows, it is widely distributed throughout our area, but seldom appears s. of 60° N.L. The introduced COMMON DANDELION, *T. officinale* Weber, has become a prevalent weed on the roadsides and waste places of parts of the Yukon, n. BC, the upper Mackenzie River valley and s. and c. Alas. Young dandelion leaves may be eaten raw or cooked as a green vegetable. The older leaves are extremely bitter. When raw, the fresh leaves are an excellent source of vitamin C and pro-vitamin A.

ILLUSTRATED GLOSSARY

1. Terms relative to UNDERGROUND PARTS:

Bulb—underground bud having fleshy scales like an onion.
Corm—vertical, thickened, solid underground stem.
Rhizome—horizontal, elongated, subterranean stem that usually has roots on the lower side and leafy stems on the upper. Characteristic of spreading plants such as many of the sedges and grasses.
Tuber—thickened, solid, underground stem with buds ("eyes") as in a potato.

2. Terms relative to STEMS:

Ascending—growing obliquely upward.
Bulbil, Bulblet—little bulb. Often produced by some plants in the axils of the leaves or replacing flowers.
Caespitose—growing in a dense tuft.
Caudex—the thickened base of a perennial plant.
Decumbent—extending along the ground, but turning upward near the end.
Erect—growing vertically.
Node—point on a stem from which leaves and/or branches arise.
Scape—leafless flowering stem rising from the ground, or from a rosette of basal leaves.
Stolon—horizontal stem running over the surface of the ground, rooting at the nodes and sometimes forming new plants.

3. Terms relative to LEAVES:

A. Arrangement and habit of leaves:

Alternate—Only one leaf at a node. Leaves originate one above the other on opposite or nearly opposite sides of the stem; not in pairs.
Cauline leaves—stem leaves.
Clasping—leaves partly surrounding the stem (e.g., most grasses).
Connate—fused.
Deciduous—plants with leaves (or flower parts) that are shed seasonally, as opposed to evergreen.
Evergreen—plants that retain their leaves throughout the year.
Imbricate—leaves or bracts arranged like shingles on a roof.
Opposite—leaves originating in pairs, opposite each other.
Persistent—leaves (or flowering parts) that remain attached after withering.
Petiolate—leaves with a petiole or stalk.
Rosette—leaves forming a ring or cluster, usually at ground level.
Sessile—leaves without a petiole or any kind of stalk.
Verticillate—leaves (or flowers) arranged in whorls.
Whorl—three or more leaves at one node, arranged wheel-like around the stem.

B. Leaf types:

Bracts—specialized leaves from the axils of which flowers arise; differing from foliage leaves in size, shape or texture, sometimes brightly coloured.

Bracteoles, Bractlet—small bracts such as those found on the pedicel of a flower.

Compound leaves—leaves with a number of leaflets from a single stalk (petiole).

  Palmately compound—leaves with three or more leaflets arising from a common centre.

  Pinnately compound—leaves like the pinnae of a feather, the leaflets arranged in pairs on opposite sides of an elongated axis.

  Bipinnately or **Tripinnately compound**—leaves that are pinnately compound 2 or 3 times over (i.e., leaflets are themselves compound) (e.g., most of the Pea Family).

  Ternate—leaves that have only 3 leaflets that may or may not be further divided.

Simple leaf—one with a single blade. The margins of the blade may be entire or variously notched or lobed, but never divided to the mid-rib.

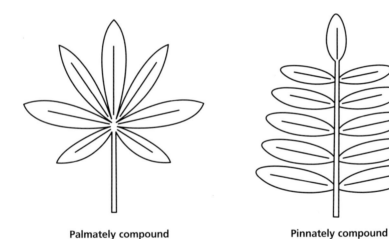

Palmately compound   Pinnately compound

Bipinnately or Tripinnately compound

C. Parts of a leaf:

1. **Blade**—expanded flat portion of a leaf.
2. **Stipule**—one of a pair of appendages often found at the base of the petiole.
3. **Axil**—point of the angle between stem and leaf, or petiole.
4. **Petiole**—stalk, or extension of the mid-rib, joining the leaf blade to the stem of the plant.

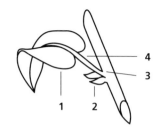

D. Shapes of leaves:

linear

lanceolate

oblanceolate

oblong

ovate

obovate

spatulate

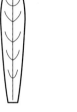
elliptical

cuneate, cuneiform

deltoid

cordate

obcordate

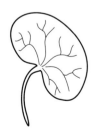
reniform

sagittate

orbicular

E. Margins of leaves:

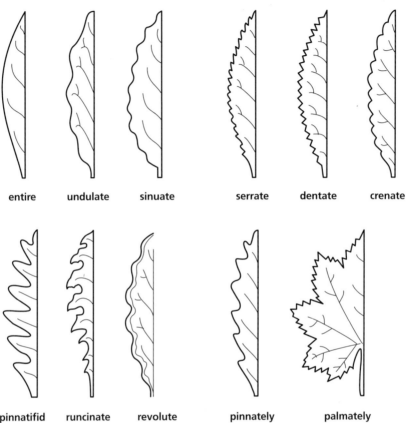

entire   undulate   sinuate   serrate   dentate   crenate

pinnatifid   runcinate   revolute   pinnately lobed   palmately lobed

F. Tips of leaves:

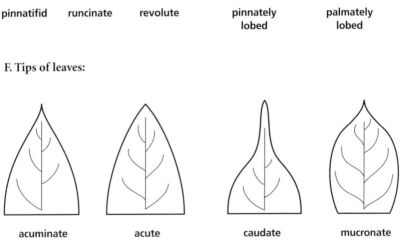

acuminate   acute   caudate   mucronate

obtuse   retuse

G. Surfaces and textures of leaves, bracts, stems, sepals and seeds:

(a) Surface textures:

Coriaceous—leathery.

Farinose—covered with a mealy powder.

Glabrate—few hairs, becoming glabrous with age.

Glabrous—lacking hairiness, smooth.

Glaucous—greyish or bluish in colour due to a thin coating of minute powdery or waxy particles (i.e., with a "bloom").

Lustrous—glossy, shiny.

Muricate—a surface having small, sharp projections.

Papillate, papillose—bearing minute, rounded projections.

Pustulate—bearing small elevations or spots resembling blisters.

Verrucose—warty, covered with low rounded protuberances.

Viscid—sticky.

(b) Degrees and types of hairiness:

Appressed—lying flat or close against a surface. Often applied to hairs.

Arachnoid—cobwebby, with thin, relatively long, interlaced hairs.

Bearded—with long stiff hairs.

Canescent—with close greyish hairiness.

Ciliate—with marginal hairs or bristles.

Crisped—a curled leaf margin or curled hairs.

Diffuse—loosely or widely spreading—often applied to hairs.

Floccose—irregularly covered by tufts of soft, woolly hair.

Glandular—bearing glands (secreting organs) usually producing nectar or volatile oil, often in the form of elongated tips of hairs; these are usually sticky.

Hirsute—with spreading, rather stiff or bristly hairs.

Hispid—with stiff or rigid, spreading hairs.

Lanate—woolly.

Pilose—with sparse, soft, straight, spreading hairs.

Plumose—feathery, having fine soft hairs along the sides.

Pubescent—covered with hairs, especially soft, downy hairs.

Sericeous—silky, with soft hairs.

Seta—a bristle.

Setaceous—bristle-like or bristle-shaped.

Setose—covered with bristles.

Stellate—star-shaped, referring to branched hairs.

Tomentose—woolly, with a covering of curly, matted hairs.

Villous—bearing long, soft hairs.

4. Terms relative to FLOWERS:

(a) Regular, "perfect" flower
(having radial symmetry and functional
male and female parts):

1. Petals—segments of **corolla.**
2. Sepals—segments of **calyx.**
3. Pedicel, peduncle—flower stalk.
4. Receptacle—part of flower stem that
supports sepals, petals, stamens and pistil.
5. Ovary
6. Style
7. Stigma
   pistil—female part
8. Filament
9. Anther
   stamen—male part.

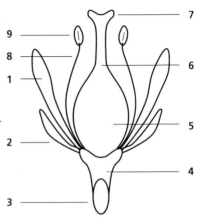

(b) Composite flower head
(inflorescence):

1. **Receptacle**—part to which all the flowers
   are attached.
2. **Involucral bract, phyllary**—bracts that
   subtend the flower head; may be
   arranged like shingles on a roof.
3. **Ray flower, ligulate flower**—the
   marginal flowers of a flower head.
4. **Tube flower, disc flower**—the central
   flowers.
5. **Pappus**—a hairy or bristly structure
   developing from the top of an **Achene** to
   assist in seed dispersal. The equivalent of
   the **Calyx** in the composites.

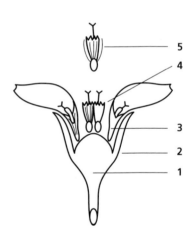

(c) Irregular flowers
(having bilateral symmetry):

(i) Orchidaceae
1. Upper sepal.
2. Two fused petals.
3. Lateral sepal.
4. Lip—third petal.
5. Stigma.
6. Anthers.
7. Spur—extension of lip.

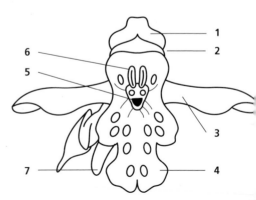

(ii) Labiatae
1. **Calyx**—5-lobed, tubular.
2. **Corolla**—upper lip (2 fused petals).
3. **Corolla**—lower lip (3 fused petals).

(iii) Leguminosae
1. **Calyx**—5-lobed, tubular.
2. **Corolla**—standard.
3. **Corolla**—wing.
4. **Corolla**—keel (2 fused petals).

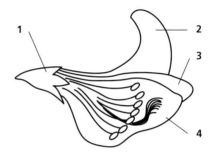

(d) Other terms relative to flowers:

Calyx—the outer part of the flower, composed of sepals.

Campanulate—shaped like a bell.

Clawed—refers to petals and sepals having a slender, stalk-like basal portion (e.g. many of the Crowfoot Family).

Corolla—the collective name for the petals.

Dioecious—a plant having flowers of only one sex, the different sexes being on separate plants.

Discoid—a composite head where no ray flowers are present.

Gamopetalous flower—having petals united, often tubular (e.g. Heath Family, Bluebell Family).

Locule—the compartment of an ovary.

Monoecious—a plant having flowers of one sex, but both kinds appear on the same plant.

Nectary—gland secreting nectar, usually on the petals or in the spur (e.g. some Orchids).

Perianth—the calyx and corolla collectively, or either one when only one is present. Used particularly when the calyx and corolla cannot easily be distinguished.

Polypetalous flower—petals separate, not united.

Salverform—a tubular corolla, that widens abruptly.

Urceolate—a tubular corolla slightly contracted at the throat, appearing urn-shaped (e.g. some members of the Heath Family).

5. Terms relative to INFLORESCENCES:

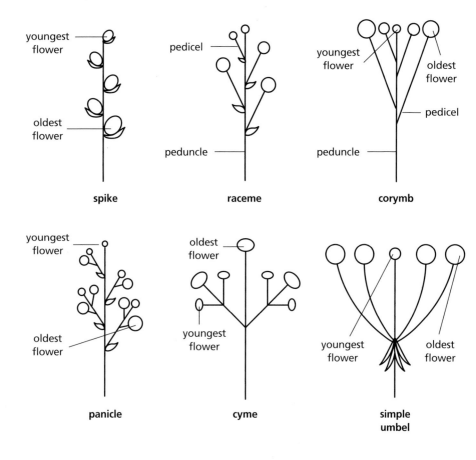

spike

raceme

corymb

panicle

cyme

simple umbel

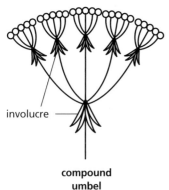

compound umbel

6. Terms relative to FRUIT:

Achene—small, nut-like, one-seeded fruit (e.g. Composite and Crowfoot families).
Aggregate fruit—fruit derived from more than one ovary (e.g. strawberry).
Beak—a thin, terminal slender tip, often found on achenes.
Capsule—dry fruit, often multi-chambered, containing two or more seeds.
Follicle—dry fruit from a single ovary, splitting on one side.
Legume—dry, one-chambered fruit from a single ovary, splitting along two sides (e.g. pea).
Loment—legume or silique with constrictions between seeds.
Silique, silicle—two-chambered fruit with a partition between two rows of seeds (found only in the Mustard Family).

7. Terms relative to WHOLE PLANT:

Herbaceous plant—a non-woody plant that dies to the ground each winter, though a dead stalk may remain.
Parasitic plant—fibrous roots are replaced by specialized structures that penetrate tissues of host plant and draw sustenance from it; often lacks chlorophyll.
Saprophytic plant—lives on dead organic matter, hence it (usually) has no need of green chlorophyll pigment.
Woody plant—a plant with stems that do not die in wintertime (trees and shrubs).

KEY TO SPECIES USING FLOWER COLOUR AND SHAPE

The species described and illustrated in this field guide are listed below according to six more or less distinct flower-colour groups as follows:

Red, Pink and Orange Flowers
Yellow Flowers
White and Cream Flowers
Blue and Violet Flowers
Green Flowers
Lilac and Purple Flowers

Within each flower-colour group the species are again grouped according to eight flower shapes, each marked with a symbol, as shown below.

1. Radially symmetrical flowers with 4 or more petals never fused for more than half their length.
e.g. Cut-leaf anemone, *Anemone multifida* p. 40

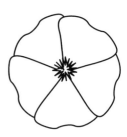

2. Radially symmetrical flowers with 3 petals and 3 sepals that are often the same colour and shape as the petals.
e.g. Elegant poison camas, *Zigadenus elegans* p. 17

3. Small, radially symmetrical flowers borne in umbels. Number of petals and sepals usually 5.
e.g. Thoroughwax, *Bupleurum americanum* p. 109

4. Radially symmetrical flowers with petals
fused for more than half their length—often
in tubular or urn-shaped structures.
e.g. Bladder campion, *Silene uralensis*
p. 34
Western moss heather, *Cassiope mertensiana*
p. 118

5. Bilaterally symmetrical flowers with petals
not fused for more than half their length.
Excluding orchid type flowers (#7).
e.g. Arctic milk-vetch, *Astragalus americanus*
p. 95

6. Bilaterally symmetrical flowers with petals
fused for more than half their length.
e.g. Langsdorf's lousewort, *Pedicularis
langsdorfii* p. 154

7. Bilaterally symmetrical flowers of the orchid
type (see illustrated glossary).
e.g. Yellow lady's slipper, *Cypripedium
parviflorum* p. 20

8. Composite flowers in "heads," often with
petal-like ray florets. The whole "head"
resembles a single flower.
e.g. Black-tipped groundsel, *Senecio lugens*
p. 187

A few species whose flowers do not easily fit
into these categories of colour and shape are
listed under the heading "Miscellaneous" at
the end of the key.

RED, PINK OR ORANGE FLOWERS

Bistort	*Polygonum bistorta* (pink) p. 29
Arctic dock	*Rumex arcticus* p. 30
Strawberry blite	*Chenopodium capitatum* (bright red) p. 31
Cut-leaf anemone	*Anemone multifida* (also purple and white forms) p. 40
Western columbine	*Aquilegia formosa* (orange-red) p. 43
Parrya	*Parrya nudicaulis* (also purple or white forms) p. 59
Roseroot	*Sedum integrifolium* p. 61
Skunk currant	*Ribes glandulosum* (sometimes white) (fruit red) p. 66
Saxifrage	*Saxifraga* (3 species) pp. 68-76
Swamp cinquefoil	*Potentilla palustris* (dark red) p. 88
Prickly rose	*Rosa acicularis* p. 90
Dwarf raspberry	*Rubus arcticus* p. 90
Fireweed	*Epilobium* (2 species) pp. 107,108
Wintergreen	*Pyrola* (2 species) pp. 113, 115
Bog cranberry	*Oxycoccus microcarpus* p. 123
Rock jasmine	*Androsace chamaejasme* (often white) p. 129
Douglasia	*Douglasia* (2 species) p. 131
Primrose	*Primula* (3 species) pp. 132-134
Alaskan phlox	*Phlox alaskensis* (may also be blue or white) p. 141

Wild chives	*Allium schoenoprasum* p. 12
Northern false asphodel	*Tofieldia coccinea* p. 15

Bladder campion	*Silene uralensis* (sometimes white) p. 34
Moss campion	*Silene acaulis* p. 35
Enchanter's nightshade	*Circaea alpina* (sometimes white) p. 106
Swamp willow-herb	*Epilobium palustre* p. 106
Bog rosemary	*Andromeda polifolia* p. 116
Bearberry	*Arctostaphylos* (2 species) pp. 116, 118
Alaska moss heather	*Harrimanella stelleriana* (usually white) p. 119
Bog laurel	*Kalmia polifolia* p. 121
Alpine azalea	*Loiseleuria procumbens* p. 122
Pink mountain heather	*Phyllodoce empetriformis* p. 124
Blueberry	*Vaccinium* (2 species) pp. 126, 127

Rock cranberry	*Vaccinium vitis-idaea* p. 128
Dogbane	*Apocynum androsaemifolium* p. 140
Twin-flower	*Linnaea borealis* p. 162
Capitate valerian	*Valeriana capitata* p. 163

Bodin's milk-vetch	*Astragalus bodinii* p. 95
Deflexed oxytrope	*Oxytropis deflexa* (also blue and white forms) p. 99

Pale corydalis	*Corydalis sempervirens* (red and yellow) p. 52
Paintbrush	*Castilleja* (3 species) pp. 148-150
Lousewort	*Pedicularis* (4 species) pp. 152-156

One-leaf orchid	*Amerorchis rotundifolia* (pink) p. 18
Calypso	*Calypso bulbosa* (pink) p. 19

Yarrow	*Achillea millefolium* (usually white) p. 167
Pink pussy-toes	*Antennaria rosea* p 169
Mountain aster	*Aster alpinus* ssp. *vierhapperi* p. 175
Fleabane daisy	*Erigeron acris* p. 179

YELLOW FLOWERS

Yellow water lily	*Nuphar polysepala* p. 37
Yellow anemone	*Anemone richardsonii* p. 42
Marsh marigold	*Caltha palustris* p. 44
Crowfoot, buttercup	*Ranunculus* (10 species) pp. 45-49
Poppy	*Papaver* (2 species) pp. 50, 51
Winter cress	*Barbarea orthoceras* p. 53
Tansy mustard	*Descurainia sophioides* (yellow-green) p. 55
Draba	*Draba* (2 species) pp. 56, 57
Yellow wallflower	*Erysimum angustatum* p. 57
Arctic bladderpod	*Lesquerella arctica* p. 58
Lance-leaved stonecrop	*Sedum lanceolatum* (pale yellow) p. 61
Golden saxifrage	*Chrysosplenium wrightii* p. 62
Mitrewort	*Mitella nuda* (yellow-green) p. 63
Saxifrage	*Saxifraga* (4 species) pp. 68-76
Yellow dryas	*Dryas drummondii* p. 77
Avens	*Geum* (3 species) pp. 80-81
Potentilla, cinquefoil	*Potentilla* (15 species) pp. 82-89
Sibbaldia	*Sibbaldia procumbens* p. 93
Silverberry	*Elaeagnus commutata* p. 105
Greenish-flowered wintergreen	*Pyrola chlorantha* (yellowish-green) p. 114

Western false asphodel	*Triantha glutinosa* (yellowish-white) p. 16

Thoroughwax	*Bupleurum americanum* p. 109

Yellow mountain heather	*Phyllodoce glanduliflora* (greenish-yellow) p. 124

Arctic milk-vetch	*Astragalus* (2 species) pp. 95, 96
Sweet clover	*Melilotus officinalis* p. 98
Locoweed, oxytrope	*Oxytropis* (3 species) pp. 99-101

Yellow corydalis	*Corydalis aurea* p. 51
Paintbrush	*Castilleja* (3 species) pp. 148-150
Common monkey flower	*Mimulus guttatus* p. 152
Lousewort	*Pedicularis* (3 species) pp. 153-155

Northern coral-root	*Corallorhiza trifida* (greenish-yellow) p. 20
Yellow lady's slipper	*Cypripedium parviflorum* p. 20

Arnica	*Arnica* (4 species) pp. 170-171
Wormwood	*Artemisia* (greenish-yellow)
	(5 species) pp. 172-175
Hawksbeard	*Crepis* (2 species) pp. 177, 178
Groundsel, butterweed	*Senecio* (10 species) pp. 185-190
Goldenrod	*Solidago* (3 species) pp. 190-191
Horned dandelion	*Taraxacum ceratophorum* p. 192

WHITE AND CREAM-COLOURED FLOWERS

HERBACEOUS

Wild rhubarb, alpine bistort	*Polygonum* (2 species) pp. 28, 29
Tuberous spring-beauty	*Claytonia tuberosa* p. 31
Mouse-ear chickweed	*Cerastium arvense* p. 32
Long-stalked starwort	*Stellaria longipes* p. 36
Anemone	*Anemone* (4 species) pp. 39-42
Mountain marsh marigold	*Caltha leptosepala* p. 44
Water crowfoot	*Ranunculus aquatilis* p. 45
Few-flowered meadowrue	*Thalictrum sparsiflorum* p. 50
Low braya	*Braya humilis* p. 53
Alpine bittercress, cuckoo flower	*Cardamine* (2 species) pp. 54, 55
Parrya	*Parrya nudicaulis* (also rose or purple forms) p. 59
Sundew	*Drosera* (2 species) p. 60
Alaska boykinia	*Boykinia richardsonii* p. 62
Leather-leaved saxifrage	*Leptarrhena pyrolifolia* p. 63
Grass-of-Parnassus	*Parnassia* (3 species) pp. 64-65
Saxifrage	*Saxifraga* (9 species) pp. 68-76
Chamaerhodos	*Chamaerhodos erecta* p. 77
Mountain avens, dryas	*Dryas* (2 species) pp. 77, 78
Wild strawberry	*Fragaria virginiana* p. 79
Partridge foot	*Luetkea pectinata* p. 82
Glandular cinquefoil	*Potentilla arguta* (sometimes yellow) p. 82
Cloudberry	*Rubus chamaemorus* p. 91
Fireweed	*Epilobium angustifolium* (usually pink) p. 107
Swamp willow-herb	*Epilobium palustre* (sometimes pink) p. 106
Single delight	*Moneses uniflora* p. 112
Arctic wintergreen	*Pyrola grandiflora* p. 115
One-sided pyrola	*Orthilia secunda* (often greenish-white) p. 115
Lapland diapensia	*Diapensia lapponica* p. 129
Pigmy flower	*Androsace septentrionalis* p. 130
Sea milk-wort	*Glaux maritima* p. 132
Northern starflower	*Trientalis arctica* p. 135
Buckbean	*Menyanthes trifoliata* p. 140
Alaskan phlox	*Phlox alaskensis* (may also be pink or blue) p. 141
Showy Jacob's ladder	*Polemonium pulcherrimum* (usually blue) p. 142
Sitka valerian	*Valeriana sitchensis* p. 164

WOODY (SHRUBS)

Red baneberry	*Actaea rubra* (fruit is red) p. 38
Skunk currant	*Ribes glandulosum* (sometimes pink, fruit red) p. 66

Northern black currant	*Ribes hudsonianum* (fruit is black) p. 66
Serviceberry	*Amelanchier alnifolia* p. 76
Wild raspberry	*Rubus idaeus* p. 90
Sitka burnet	*Sanguisorba canadensis* (greenish-white) p. 92
Western mountain ash	*Sorbus scopulina* p. 93
Beauverd's spiraea	*Spiraea beauverdiana* p. 94
Enchanter's nightshade	*Circaea alpina* (also sometimes pink) p. 106
Dogwood	*Cornus* (2 species) pp. 110, 111
Northern Labrador tea	*Ledum palustre* p. 120
Red elderberry	*Sambucus racemosa* p. 161

Alpine lily	*Lloydia serotina* p. 13
Clasping twisted stalk	*Streptopus amplexifolius* p. 14
Star-flowered Solomon's seal	*Maianthemum stellatum* p. 15
Scotch asphodel, false asphodel	*Tofieldia* (2 species) pp. 15, 16
Elegant poison camas	*Zigadenus elegans* p. 17

Northern hemlock-parsley	*Sium suave* p. 109
Cow parsnip	*Heracleum maximum* p. 110

Bladder campion	*Silene uralensis* (sometimes pink) p. 34
Pink campion	*Silene repens* p. 36
Alpine bearberry	*Arctostaphylos alpina* p. 116
Heather	*Cassiope* (3 species) pp. 118-119
Leather-leaf	*Chamaedaphne calyculata* p. 120
Whitish gentian	*Gentiana algida* p. 136

Late yellow locoweed	*Oxytropis campestris* (often yellowish) p. 99
Deflexed oxytrope	*Oxytropis deflexa* (usually blue) p. 99
Eyebright	*Euphrasia subarctica* p. 151

Sparrow's egg lady's slipper	*Cypripedium passerinum* p. 21
Bog orchid	*Platanthera* (2 species) pp. 23, 24
Hooded ladies' tresses	*Spiranthes romanzoffiana* p. 25

Yarrow	*Achillea millefolium* (occasionally pink) p. 167
Pearly everlasting	*Anaphalis margaritacea* p. 168
Showy everlasting	*Antennaria pulcherrima* p. 169
Fleabane	*Erigeron* (3 species) pp. 179-181
Coltsfoot	*Petasites palmatus* p. 184

BLUE AND VIOLET FLOWERS

Pasque-flower	*Pulsatilla ludoviciana* (also purple form) p. 41
Blue columbine	*Aquilegia brevistyla* p. 42
Wild flax	*Linum lewisii* p. 102
Alaskan phlox	*Phlox alaskensis* (also pink and white forms) p. 141
Jacob's ladder	*Polemonium* (3 species) pp. 141-142
Scorpion-weed	*Phacelia franklinii* p. 143
Arctic forget-me-not	*Eritrichium* (2 species) pp. 144, 145
Alpine forget-me-not	*Myosotis asiatica* p. 146
Yukon bellflower	*Campanula aurita* p. 165

Blue-eyed grass	*Sisyrinchium montanum* p. 18

Gentian	*Gentiana* (4 species) p. 136-138
Tall lungwort	*Mertensiana paniculata* p. 146
Harebell	*Campanula* (2 species) pp. 165, 166

Northern monkshood	*Aconitum delphiniifolium* p. 38
Tall delphinium	*Delphinium glaucum* p. 45
Alpine milk-vetch	*Astragalus alpinus* p. 94
Arctic lupine	*Lupinus arcticus* p. 97
Deflexed oxytrope	*Oxytropis deflexa* (also white and pink forms) p. 99
Violet	*Viola* (3 species) pp. 103-104
Brooklime	*Veronica americana* p. 158
Alpine speedwell	*Veronica wormskjoldii* p. 159
Butterwort	*Pinguicula* (2 species) p. 160

Few-flowered corydalis	*Corydalis pauciflora* p. 52
Skullcap	*Scutellaria galericulata* p. 147
Lagotis	*Lagotis glauca* p. 151
Penstemon	*Penstemon* (2 species) pp. 156, 157

GREEN FLOWERS

Red-fruited bastard toad-flax	*Comandra livida* (fruit orange-red) p. 27
Tansy mustard	*Descurainia sophioides* (yellowish-green) p. 55
Wild gooseberry	*Ribes oxyacanthoides* (purplish-black fruit) p. 67
Stiff-stemmed saxifrage	*Saxifraga hieracifolia* (greenish-purple) p. 72
Sitka burnet	*Sanguisorba canadensis* (greenish-white) p. 92
Soopolallie	*Shepherdia canadensis* (fruit reddish-yellow) p. 105
Greenish-flowered wintergreen	*Pyrola chlorantha* p. 114
One-sided pyrola	*Orthilia secunda* (often greenish-white) p. 115

Scotch asphodel	*Tofieldia pusilla* (greenish-white) p. 16
False hellebore	*Veratrum eschscholtzii* p. 17

Northern coral-root	*Corallorhiza trifida* (greenish-yellow) p. 20
Green-flowered bog orchid	*Platanthera hyperborea* p. 24
Northern twayblade	*Listera borealis* p. 22
Heart-leaf twayblade	*Listera cordata* (also purple form) p. 23

LILAC AND PURPLE FLOWERS

Cut-leaf anemone	*Anemone multifida* (also cream and pink forms) p. 40
Pasque-flower	*Pulsatilla ludoviciana* (also blue form) p. 41
Cuckoo flower	*Cardamine pratensis* (sometimes white) p. 54
Purple cress	*Cardamine purpurea* p. 55
Pallas' wallflower	*Erysimum pallasii* p. 58
Parrya	*Parrya nudicaulis* (also pink and white forms) p. 59
Smelowskia	*Smelowskia borealis* p. 59
Northern red currant	*Ribes triste* (fruit red) p. 68
Stiff-stemmed saxifrage	*Saxifraga hieracifolia* (greenish-purple) p. 72
Common burnet	*Sanguisorba officinalis* (purplish-black) p. 92
Crowberry	*Empetrum nigrum* (fruit purplish-black) p. 103
Lapland rosebay	*Rhododendron lapponicum* p. 125
Northern shooting star	*Dodecatheon frigidum* p. 130

Indian rice	*Fritillaria camschatcensis* p. 13

Felwort	*Gentiana acuta* p. 136

Liquorice-root	*Hedysarum alpinum* p. 96
Northern sweet-vetch	*Hedysarum boreale* p. 97
Crazyweed, locoweed	*Oxytropis* (3 species) pp. 99-101

Gorman's penstemon	*Penstemon gormanii* (ranging from blue to purple) p. 156
Ground cone	*Boschniakia rossica* p. 159

Pink lady's slipper	*Cypripedium guttatum* p. 21
Heart-leaf twayblade	*Listera cordata* (also green form) p. 23

Aster	*Aster* (2 species) pp. 175, 176
Saussurea	*Saussurea angustifolia* p. 184

MISCELLANEOUS

Seaside arrow-grass	*Triglochin maritima* p. 11
White cotton grass	*Eriophorum scheuchzeri* p. 11
Fox-tail barley	*Hordeum jubatum* p. 12
Arctic willow	*Salix arctica* p. 25
Mountain alder	*Alnus crispa* p. 26
Sweet gale	*Myrica gale* p. 26

R. Frisch:
p. 13 bottom, p.15 bottom,
p. 20 bottom,
p. 21 middle, bottom,
p. 27 top, p. 32 bottom,
p. 34 top left, bottom,
p. 36 top, p. 37 top,
p. 38 top, p. 39 both,
p. 40 bottom, p. 41 top,
p. 45 top left,
p. 54 top, bottom left,
p. 58 top,
p. 59 top left, bottom,
p. 62 top left, bottom,
p. 65 top, p. 66 bottom,
p. 68 both
p. 70 top left, bottom,
p. 71 top,
p. 72 top, bottom left,
p. 73 top right, p. 74 top left,
p. 75 both, p. 76 top left,
p. 80 both, p. 81 bottom,
p. 82 top, p. 84 bottom,
p. 85 top, bottom left,
p. 86 bottom, p. 89 top,
p. 91 both, p. 92 top right,
p. 98 bottom, p. 100 top,
p. 107 top, p. 108 both,
p. 113, p. 117 bottom,
p. 122 top,
p. 125 top left and right,
p. 127 top, p. 129 top,
p. 130 bottom left,
p. 131 top right,
p. 134 bottom,
p. 136 bottom right,
p. 138 bottom left, p. 141 all,
p. 142 top, p. 143 bottom,
p. 144 bottom, p. 145 top,
p. 146 bottom, p. 149 top,
p. 152 bottom, p. 154 bottom,
p. 155 top, p. 159 bottom,
p. 163 bottom right,
p. 166 top, p. 167 all,
p. 168 bottom, p. 170 top,
p. 171 top, p. 174 top,
p. 177 bottom, p. 178,
p. 180 bottom, p. 181 bottom,
p. 183 bottom right,
p. 185 bottom left,
p. 187 bottom, p. 189 top,
p. 190 top,

J.G. Trelawny
p. 12 bottom,
p. 16 bottom right,
p. 17 bottom,
p. 18 top, p. 24 top,
p. 27 middle, p. 28 top,
p. 29 bottom, p. 30,
p. 31 top left, bottom,
p. 35 top, p. 40 top right,
p. 42 top and bottom,
p. 43 bottom,
p. 46 top, p. 50 top,
p. 51 top and bottom,
p. 54 bottom right,
p. 55 bottom, p. 57 bottom,

p. 61 top, p. 69 top left,
p. 78 top, p. 81 top, middle,
p. 82 middle, bottom,
p. 83 both, p. 84 top,
p. 86 top, p. 87 both,
p. 90 bottom left,
p. 92 bottom left,
p. 93 top, bottom,
p. 94 bottom, p. 95 top,
p. 96 bottom, p. 98 top left,
p. 99 bottom, p. 100 bottom,
p. 101 top, bottom,
p. 102 bottom,
p. 105 middle,
p. 106 bottom left,
p. 109 top,
p. 112 top, p. 116 bottom,
p. 117 top, p. 118 bottom
p. 121 bottom,
p. 126, p. 127 bottom,
p. 128 bottom, p. 133,
p. 135 top, p. 136 bottom left,
p. 138 top left, bottom right,
p. 142 bottom left,
p. 143 top left and right,
p. 145 bottom, p. 146 top,
p. 147 bottom,
p. 148 middle,bottom,
p. 149 bottom,
p. 150 top left, bottom,
p. 151 bottom, p. 152 top,
p. 156 bottom left and right,
p. 157 top, p. 160 bottom,
p. 161 bottom right,
p. 163 top, p. 164 top right,
p. 165 bottom, p. 167 top,
p. 171 bottom, p. 172 bottom,
p. 176 top, p. 179 bottom,
p. 182 bottom,
p. 185 top, bottom right,
p. 187 top, p. 188 both,
p. 189 bottom, p. 190 bottom,
p. 191 bottom,

W.K. Dobson
P. 11 top,
p. 16 top, bottom left,
p. 17 top left,
p. 18 bottom right,
p. 20 top, p. 22 bottom,
p. 23 all
p. 24 bottom left and right,
p. 25 top, p. 32 top,
p. 33 bottom,
p. 36 bottom,
p. 38 bottom right,
p. 40 top left, p. 44 top,
p. 49 bottom, p. 52 bottom,
p. 53 top, p. 57 top,
p. 60 top, p. 63 all,
p. 64 right, p. 66 top,
p. 69 bottom, p. 76 bottom,
p. 77 top, p. 79 top,
p. 88 top, bottom,
p. 92 top left, bottom right,
p. 93 middle, p. 94 top,
p. 99 top, p. 100 middle,
p. 101 middle, p. 103 bottom left,

p. 104 top, p. 106 bottom right,
p. 107 bottom,
p. 110 top and bottom,
p. 112 bottom,
p. 114 all, p. 115 all,
p. 116 top, p. 118 top left,
p. 131 bottom,
p. 134 top, p. 136 top,
p. 137 bottom, p. 138 top right,
p. 140 bottom, p. 142 bottom right,
p. 145 middle, p. 146 middle,
p. 147 middle, 148 top,
p. 150 middle
p. 153 top, bottom right,
p. 159 top,p. 163 middle,
p. 161 top and bottom left,
p. 164 top left,p. 165 top
p. 166 bottom,
p. 168 top and middle,
p. 169 middle and bottom,
p. 170 bottom,
p. 172 top, p. 175 top right,
p. 179 top, p. 182 top,
p. 184 bottom, p. 191 top,

N. Barichello
p. 21 top, p. 27 bottom,
p. 29 top, p. 31 top left,
p. 34 top right, p. 35 bottom,
p. 37 middle, p. 41 bottom,
p. 43 top, p. 44 bottom,
p. 45 top right,
p. 52 top left and right,
p. 55 top, p. 58 bottom,
p. 59 top right, p. 61 bottom,
p. 62 top right, p. 65 bottom,
p. 69 top right,
p. 72 top left, bottom,
p. 74 top right, bottom,
p. 77 bottom, p. 78 bottom,
p. 90 top, bottom right,
p. 96 top,
p. 97 bottom left and right,
p. 102 top, p. 105 bottom,
p. 111 top, p. 116 middle,
p. 118 top right, p. 119 bottom,
p. 120 middle and bottom,
p. 123 bottom,
p. 124 top left, bottom,
p. 125 bottom, p. 128 top,
p. 129 bottom left and right,
p. 130 bottom right,
p. 131 top left, p. 137 middle,
p. 144 top, p. 146 middle,
p. 153 bottom left,
p. 154 top left and right,
p. 155 top, p. 156 top,
p. 157 bottom,
p. 162 top, p. 163 bottom left,
p. 175 top left, p. 183 bottom,
p. 186,

T. and S. Armstrong
p. 14 all,p. 15 top, middle,
p. 28 bottom, p. 45 bottom,
p. 48 bottom, p. 85 bottom right,
p. 88 middle, p. 103 bottom right,
p. 132 top, p. 147 top,

p. 158 both, p. 175 bottom,
p. 176 middle and bottom,
p. 184 top,

G. Allen
p. 11 bottom, p. 12 top,
p. 13 top right, p. 18 bottom left,
p. 38 bottom left,
p. 47 bottom, p. 56 top,
p. 64 left, p. 71 bottom,
p. 72 bottom right,
p. 89 bottom, p. 106 top
p. 121 top, p. 132 bottom,
p. 162 bottom, p. 164 bottom,
p. 177 top, p. 181 top,

J.E. Lort
p. 13 top left, p. 25 bottom,
p. 46 bottom, p. 47 top,
p. 97 top, p. 105 top,
p. 124 middle, p. 131 middle,
p. 140,

H. Roemer
p. 17 top right,
p. 33 top, p. 37 bottom,
p. 48 top, p. 123 top,
p. 135 bottom, p. 173 top,
p. 183 top right,

Wm. J. Merilees
p. 22 top left and right,
p. 26 top and middle,
p. 67 top, middle, bottom,
p. 111 bottom, p. 130 top,

N. and R. Turner
p. 79 bottom,
p. 103 top left and right,

R. VanDalen
p. 26 bottom, p. 120 top,

J. A. Antos
p. 60 bottom,

V. Pratt
p. 49 top, p. 119 top,
p. 137, p. 160 top

M. Barker
p. 50 bottom, p. 139

B. Bennett
p. 53 bottom, p. 95 bottom,
p. 109 bottom, p. 192,

J.M. Woollett
p. 19 top and bottom,
p. 151 top,

J. Pojar
p. 56 bottom

T.C. Brayshaw
p. 180 top,

CLARK, LEWIS J. (author) and J.G. TRELAWNY (editor): *Wild Flowers of the Pacific Northwest*, Gray's Publishing Ltd., Sidney, BC. 1976.

CODY, W.J.: *Flora of the Yukon Territory*, NRC Research Press, Ottawa. 1996.

CORMACK, R.G.H.: *Wild Flowers of Alberta*, Hurtig Publishers, Edmonton. 1977.

DOUGLAS, W. GEORGE, et al.: *The Rare Vascular Plants of the Yukon*, National Museums of Canada, Ottawa. 1981.

EPPS, ALAN C: *Wild Edible and Poisonous Plants of Alaska*, Publication No. 28, Cooperative Extension Service, University of Alaska. 1976.

HEILER, CHRISTINE A.: *Wild Flowers of Alaska*, Graphic Arts Centre, Portland, Oregon. 1966.

HITCHCOCK, C. LEO and ARTHUR CRONQUIST: *Flora of the Pacific Northwest*, University of Washington Press, Seattle. 1973.

HULTÉN, ERIC: *Flora of Alaska and Neighboring Territories*, Stanford University Press, Stanford, California. 1968.

KINGSBURY, JOHN M.: *Poisonous Plants of the United States and Canada*, Prentice-Hall, NJ. 1964.

PORSILD, A.E.: *Botany of Southeastern Yukon adjacent to the Canol Road*, National Museum of Canada, Bulletin No. 121, Ottawa. 1951.

PORSILD, A.E.: *Edible Roots and Berries of Northern Canada*, National Museum of Canada, Ottawa. 1937.

PORSILD, A.E.: *Rocky Mountain Wild Flowers*, National Museum of Canada, Ottawa. 1974.

PORSILD, A.E. and WILLIAM J. CODY: *Vascular Plants of Continental Northwest Territories*, National Museum of Canada, Ottawa. 1980.

SHARPLES, ADA W.: *Alaska Wild Flowers*, Stanford University Press, Stanford, California. 1958.

WELSH, STANLEY L.: *Anderson's Flora of Alaska and adjacent parts of Canada*, Brigham Young University Press, Provo, Utah. 1974.

WHITE, HELEN A. and MAXINE WILLIAMS (editors): *The Alaska–Yukon Wild Flower Guide*, Alaska Northwest Publishing Company, Anchorage, Alaska. 1974.

Additional Field Guides from Harbour Publishing

Wild Flowers of Field & Slope by Lewis Clark
5.5" x 8.5" • 80 pages, 100 colour photos
1-55017-255-7 • $9.95
The first in the reprinted series of Lewis Clark's bestselling wild flower field guides, perfect for gardeners, hikers and nature lovers.

Wild Flowers of Forest & Woodland by Lewis Clark
5.5" x 8.5" • 80 pages, 100 colour photos
1-55017-306-5 • $12.95
A new addition in the reprinted series of Lewis Clark's bestselling wild flower field guides, perfect for gardeners, hikers and nature lovers.

Wild Flowers of the Mountains by Lewis Clark
5.5" x 8.5" • 80 pages, 100 colour photos
1-55017-308-1 • $12.95
Another addition in the reprinted series of Lewis Clark's bestselling wild flower field guides, perfect for gardeners, hikers and nature lovers.

Pacific Reef and Shore: A Photo Guide to Northwest Marine Life by Rick M. Harbo
5.5" x 8.5" • 80 pages, 300 colour photos
1-55017-304-9 • $9.95
This handy full-colour field guide to the marine life of coastal British Columbia, Alaska, Washington, Oregon and northern California is perfect for divers, boaters, beachwalkers and snorkellers. It is the successor to Harbo's 1980 bestseller *Tidepool and Reef.*

Whelks to Whales: Coastal Marine Life of the Pacific Northwest by Rick M. Harbo
5.5" x 8.5" • 248 pages, 500 colour photos
1-55017-183-6 • $24.95
This award-winning field guide features full-colour photos of the 420 most common species of coastal British Columbia, Alaska, Washington, Oregon and northern California. Entries include comprehensive but concise information on size, range, habitat and facts of interest about each species.

Shells and Shellfish of the Pacific Northwest by Rick M. Harbo
5.5" x 8.5" • 272 pages, 350 colour photos
1-55017-146-1 • $24.95
This easy-to-follow, full-colour guide introduces more than 250 species of mollusks found along the beaches and shallow waters of the Pacific Northwest.

The Beachcomber's Guide to Seashore Life in the Pacific Northwest by J. Duane Sept
5.5" x 8.5" • 240 pages, 500 colour photos
1-55017-204-2 • $21.95
274 of the most common animals and plants found along the saltwater shores of the
Pacific Northwest are described in this book. Illustrating each entry is a colour
photo of the species in its natural habitat.

Pacific Seaweeds: A Guide to Common Seaweeds of the West Coast by Louis Druehl
5.5" x 8.5" • 192 pages, 80 colour photos, illustrations
1-55017-240-9 • $24.95
The authoritative guide to over 100 common species of seaweed. Includes
interesting facts, scientific information and tasty recipes.

West Coast Fossils by Rolf Ludvigsen and Graham Beard
5.5" x 8.5" • 216 pages, 250 photos, illustrations and maps
1-55017-179-8 • $18.95
This complete new and expanded edition of a West Coast classic is a concise and
thorough guide to the small and large fossils of Vancouver Island and the Gulf
Islands of Canada.